NEW PATTERNS OF WORK

NEW PATTERNS OF WORK

Edited by Hugh Ormiston and Donald M Ross

SCOTTISH CHURCHES' INDUSTRIAL MISSION

First published in 1990 by The Saint Andrew Press on behalf of
Scottish Churches' Industrial Mission and the Board for Social Responsibility
of the Church of England, with kind assistance from Church
House Publishing.

British Library Cataloguing in Publication Data
New patterns of work.
 1. Work patterns
 331.257

  ISBN 0–86153–127–2

This book is set in Times Roman.

Typeset by J&L Composition Ltd, Filey, North Yorkshire.

Printed and Bound in Great Britain by
Athenaeum Press Ltd., Newcastle upon Tyne.

Contents

Preface

At a time of fairly major change in patterns of working, this book is produced with a number of purposes in mind. First, we believe that while these changes are by no means imperceptible, they are almost surreptitious by nature. It is clear even to the casual observer that the large employers of labour forces of thousands have been replaced in the eighties by much smaller enterprises employing far fewer blue collar workers and often many more part-time workers. We believe, however, there is a case to be made for raising the general awareness of these changes, the motivating forces behind them and the implications for society at large. Second, it follows from this that there is a need to stimulate much more discussion about the nature of changes in work life and patterns of employment so that the changes may be better understood and the consequences foreseen. Third, we hope that by raising awareness and stimulating discussion this little book will in some very small measure contribute to the induction of a move to more just practices in the employment of people in contemporary society. We make no apology for stating this motive at the outset. Our perspective on the world of work is from the insights of the Christian Church. We regard work life as of fundamental importance, not only for the satisfaction of a range of personal needs, but for the survival of the human family and the environment in which it lives. One of our fundamental concerns therefore is always our regard for the just order of that society, that ultimately all may benefit, none be marginalised, and thus the hope of the Kingdom better realised.

More specifically, our interest as church people arises from several decades of Industrial Mission activity throughout Britain. During this time there has been a long history of close contact between the churches and industry through the shifting pattern of closures, redundancies, new developments and the restructuring of industry. These have given rise on the Church's part to Redundancy Survival Kits, programmes of preparation for redundancy, Church Action with the Unemployed, the Church of

Scotland's Society, Religion and Technology Project, Church of
Scotland General Assembly and other Church statements. These
have been accompanied by 15 years of involvement with Government programmes, including Job Creation and the Manpower
Services Commission, and numerous pamphlets and booklets on
almost every aspect of industrial life. In all of this a certain concern
has been human relationships in the workplace, which are but part
of the wider network of human relations to which all of us belong.
Their importance is appreciated by all the world faiths, but is of
particular concern for Christians who have been enjoined to love
their neighbour as themselves. Specifically, we view with particular
interest the demise of large employers of labour in favour of small
labour forces, less structured, more flexible, perhaps more egali-
tarian. We note the emphasis this puts on the initial acquisition of
skills and the need for continuous retraining. We note also the
more difficult position of those who, for one reason or another,
cannot acquire apposite skills and are therefore marginalised, but
that is the subject of another, though related, debate.

There is a sense in which our interest is not so much in what
working patterns have emerged, but rather in how they have
emerged. The how often seems determined by economic forces
rather than by rational forethought. In this there have clearly been
winners and losers. Our concern as Church people is that the
number of winners is maximised on the basis of the great com-
mandment, "Love your Neighbour". Consequently, as observers
of contemporary trends in the organisation of work, we ask what
effect are the changes having on individual employees? Are they
essentially dehumanising, manipulative, exploitative, dangerous
and atomising, or are they stimulating, liberating, creative, and
pushing people to new maturities and responsibilities? For employees reared in a culture of employment by others, employment
in large or small secure firms offering long-term, regular, even life-
long opportunities of the use of skills, development of career and
steady progress towards rewarding pensionable retirement, the
new era may indeed be traumatic. Many formerly living and
working in an employment culture now find themselves in a
culture of self-empowerment, of personal enterprise, of self-
sufficiency and of self-reliance. Where formerly life planning
implied security of work in a job provided by others, new life
planning seems inevitably to place the responsibility on the
individual and perhaps the individual in a community wider than
the work group. While for many these fundamental changes must
be disturbing, we in the Church remain convinced that God's will
can be done on the other side of change and that human resilience

and creativity can modify the dehumanising aspects of the new regime in favour of a more just and life-enhancing system.

An Institute of Personal Management study on flexible employment led to the conclusion that most changes in working patterns had not created employment, though they had spread the available work. Against this background it is difficult to discover what the aspirations of workers really are. Many may wish to work in the new pattern of flexible, temporary or sub-contract employment. It is known to be largely favoured by substantial numbers of female workers. It could, however, be argued that the very features which make part-time and temporary working attractive to employers — freedom to lay off staff, lower levels of fringe benefits, etc — must, by definition, make it a less desirable pattern of work from the worker's point of view.

What is not in doubt is the basic significance of regular work. It is more than earning a living. It imposes a time structure on the day, week, month or year, and ensures regular contact and shared experience with people outside the family, and points to goals and purposes beyond the scope of the individual. Furthermore, it grants a status of position in life, and identity, and ensures that the individual becomes and remains active in mind and body and spirit. In other words, it makes him part of wider life. Work thus contributes to the sense of personal being. It is no accident that it is perpetually surrounded by a number of fundamental questions. Who am I? What am I? What have I been? What shall I become? Who accepts me? To what group will I belong in two, five or ten years time? Thus we believe the issues in this book to be of legitimate theological concern.

> "Through work man must earn his daily bread and contribute to the continual advance of science and technology and above all to elevating unceasingly the cultural and moral level of the society within which he lives in community with those who belong to the same family."

With that statement of the Pope in 1981 all Christians can agree. Whatever else may be said about the Kingdom of God, it is most certainly in this world. Through the world of work the history of that Kingdom is shaped, and the quality of life for individuals and communities inevitably determined.

Our hope therefore is that this booklet will be widely read for what it is, a stimulus to thought and discussion. Our hope is that changes in working practice may not simply be left to market forces but be subject to careful thought and planning, and judiciously introduced with the consent of the majority. Furthermore, our hope is that Europe, the cradle of the Industrial Revolution, may not simply continue to export industrialism, but accept the role of pacesetter in good working practices and serve as a model for the world. In this respect it may eliminate the need for developing countries to pass through some of the worst features of industrial evolution and help create a world of socially useful, honest endeavour in conditions that maximise human dignity.

Finally, our thanks to the contributors. While they are each experts in their fields, they have laboured long and diligently to produce the papers which appear in this book. As is usual with the Church, they give of their labour willingly, knowing that there may be little personal gain in so doing, but that they make a contribution to the welfare of the whole.

It is inevitable in a fast-changing world that delay in publication may have made some comments less immediately topical.

HUGH ORMISTON
DONALD M ROSS
Scottish Churches' Industrial Mission

Foreword

This set of papers deals with matters that are of great significance. There is much more to life than work. But what we work at, how it is organised, where and in what conditions we undertake it, and how it is valued are all crucial to us as individuals. Moreover, by our work we shape societies, build our nations and develop our world.

The changes indicated in these pages present both threat and opportunity. There are dangers that the changes may create imbalances and make for deeper injustice. There are however opportunities for Christians and others to arrange better our work and our work-relationships and so build a better order.

The life situation, employment security, and career expectations for many people have vastly changed in recent years. I certainly recognise the shift from the period when in our towns and cities one or two major companies were the employers of many thousands of people who could expect full time and regular employment, agreed working conditions, regular holiday entitlement, long term prospects and a steady move through life to retirement. Now large numbers of people are part of the many small companies which provide goods and services, or are self employed, or are in some temporary form of work relationship, and who know little of such earlier securities. This is no doubt stimulating for some, but it does make others vulnerable and raises questions about the public and private policy decisions which have to be made.

I am happy to commend the study of this document to Christians and all others concerned about these changes. The Church of England's Board for Social Responsibility has long been associated with Industrial Mission, which has itself had a long experience of ecumenical co-operation, not least with our colleagues of the Scottish Churches'Industrial Mission.

THE RIGHT REVD JOHN YATES
Bishop of Gloucester

1

Sub-Contracting in Context: Labour Flexibility in British Industry

The practice of sub-contracting is as old as work itself. Employers with more work than they can handle naturally turn their thoughts to "putting work out". Historically, there have even been cases where the entire output of an industry has been organised on the basis of sub-contracting — as in the medieval cloth trade, or later in the homes of cotton workers before they were gathered into factories as permanent employees. In coal mining, sub-contracting took the form of the notorious "butty" system which held down labour costs (therefore wages) and lasted well into this century. There are even now fears that it may yet return as deregulation of the industry works it way down to the level of the pit. Nor is sub-contracting necessarily a marginal economic activity. Large sectors of modern, industrialised economies are organised in this way, perhaps most notably in Japan. There, large corporations and small sub-contractors maintain a mutually dependent relationship, but in the context of inferior pay, conditions and job security in the small firms sector which remains important in employment terms: establishments with less than 100 workers comprise about 60% of all Japanese employment.[1]

British employers, as in other industrialised economies, have for long found advantages in sub-contracting. However, whilst important in itself, it is more usefully seen as one aspect of the pursuit of labour flexibility by employers. Exclusive concentration upon sub-contracting may direct attention away from the much wider phenomenon which is currently attracting widespread attention from policymakers and commentators as well as employers, and is of major significance for those at the receiving end of innnovations in flexible working. Additionally, we now have available a major piece of recent research on sub-contracting in the UK.[2]

Current interest in labour flexibility is itself an aspect of a long concern in Britain about labour utilisation. This has taken two forms: reducing the size of labour forces and increasing the productivity of the remainder. Even with lower output levels, productivity will increase if the fall in the labour force is proportionately greater than the fall in output. This arithmetical 'solution' is paid for in lost output, lost jobs and an increased burden upon unemployment and social security funding. Yet shrinking employment is often used as an indicator of industrial virility and progress.

The other approach to productivity improvement and reducing labour costs per unit of output is through measures to increase the flexibility of the workforce. This is not a recent development. The current vogue in organisations for ways of increasing labour flexibility is reminiscent of the productivity bargaining fashion of the sixties.[3] This was strongly encouraged by the then Labour Government and the National Board for Prices and Incomes in the belief that it would help to improve the supposedly inferior productivity performance of British workers. The favoured approach was a comprehensive plant productivity agreement in which shop stewards agreed to a blurring of traditional job demarcations, greater flexibility in the deployment of labour, and the surrendering of restrictive practices in return for substantial increases in pay and, commonly, employment guarantees. This last was not in any case a problem in a period of high employment and still great expectations.

Most of these high hopes were not realised, partly because most productivity gains were bogus, concocted jointly by management and unions to evade the Government's controls on pay increases. These contexts and circumstances have disappeared but there is still something to be gained from shining a light back into this period to help to assess the durability, value and ethical basis of current industrial relations fashions and experiments. The *contexts* of productivity bargaining and drive for greater labour flexibility are, of course, completely different. Trade union negotiators (normally shop stewards) and management were bargaining in the sixties against a background of a still strong industrial base, full employment, a well-established industrial relations culture and public policies which conferred legitimacy upon trade unions, albeit 'responsible' ones. Nor was it thought proper, at government level, to promote different shift-working patterns without looking at their human consequences. The physiological and social effects on workers' health and well-being of rotating shift patterns were widely seen as a 'cost' which had to be placed alongside the benefits. An economic, social and medical appraisal of hours of work, overtime and shiftwork was in fact the part subject of a major NBPI report.[4]

Time and change have also made their marks. It is no longer axiomatic to complain that the work performance of the British is inferior[5] to their counterparts in other countries. The productivity claims of certain industries, although in size much smaller than twenty years ago, are now strong — notably steel, cars, coalmining and (prior to its virtual recent disappearance) merchant shipbuilding. The fate of shipbuilding should warn us — but probably will not — that productivity gains are hollow if an industry falls off the graph. Here *size* can be critical. For example in Scotland James Burroughs plc is up for sale because it is seemingly not big enough to compete (despite good products and a well-managed enterprise) with the elaborate distribution and marketing networks of the big, international players. In England, Jaguar is about to be bought by Ford partly because it is too small — a fate which must soon befall the Rover Group, the last domino in a once full set.

These past and present differences and wider perspectives need to be kept in view in considerations of labour flexibility in all its forms. Labour flexibility also raises ethical considerations. One of these, which has already been alluded to, concerns the effects of more flexible shift patterns on the health and well-being of workers. Another is that attempts to reduce unit labour costs through greater flexibility implicitly place the blame and burden for poor performance upon trade unions and workers and frequently involve substantial job losses. Particularly since 1945, although the record can be traced back much earlier, British trade unions and workers have been repeatedly identified by management, academics and government as primarily responsible for the country's failings in economic growth and attempts to achieve external balance and price stability. More recently, workers have also been told that they cause their own unemployment. Here it must be asked how far deteriorating unit labour costs are explained by declining or stagnant output as well as the contribution to overall costs and profit performance from non-labour costs and adverse exchange rate movements — all variables almost entirely, under present institutions, outside the influence of labour. It has to be said that this lack of acceptable objectivity in the analysis is serious enough in itself, but is also unlikely to induce a willing acquiescence of workers and unions in change.

This is the climate in which managements are enthusiastically introducing flexible labour practices. Nor are they a guaranteed panacea. British industrial relations and managerial history is heavy with a succession of "breakthroughs" spawning extravagant claims and expensive conferences, but suffering those early demises which may be the fate of present enthusiasms. Labour flexibility in some, if not all its forms, *may* have lasting benefits but these should not be taken at face value and, in particular, the benefits carry costs in human as well as economic terms. It needs, as everything, to be subjected to a careful examination of its nature, assumptions and implications. Hence the remainder of this paper briefly reviews the meaning of labour flexibility, assesses its extent and offers an appraisal of its significance.

The meaning of Labour Flexibility

The concept of labour flexibility is, of course, far from new and long predates the productivity arrangements of the sixties. In its task of functional flexibility variant it challenges job demarcations, especially of traditional crafts. The history of strong trade union resistance to this process must primarily be seen as a legitimate defence of jobs and livelihoods. However, in current collective arrangements it is now commonplace for the numbers of grades to be drastically reduced and grade lines crossed by multi-skilling provisions associated with the necessary training and re-training. Such a process may be beneficial to the workers concerned within a firm, but can deepen the "duality" of the workforce in which workers are permanently divided by training, skill, security, pay, status and even unionisation. Attempts by management to achieve greater flexibility have been conceptualised in the "flexible firm"* with its concentric circles of "core" permanent workers, "periphery" of temporary and part-time workers and an outer ring of "external" contract labour. Within the flexible firm, labour can therefore be seen in four dimensions.**

- flexibility of function or task involving the creation of dual or multi-skilled craftsmen, the merging of production grades or general mobility between maintenance and production work.
- flexibility of time involving the traditional practice of overtime, flexitime, greater experimentation with shift patterns, "nine-day fortnights" and the more radical concept of annual hours.
- flexibility of numbers, that is of peripheral workers employed as part-timers and temporaries, and including YTS trainees, supplemented by the use of sub-contracted workers for specialist and contracted-out services, some of whom may be self-employed.

* *The concept of the flexible firm and the classifications of flexible labour originated in the work of John Atkinson and his colleagues at the Institute of Manpower Studies, University of Sussex.*
** *A fifth dimension, often added in trade union discussions, is flexibility of pay, eg two or three year pay deals, share ownership schemes, profit sharing performance-related pay and merit payments.*

• changes in the pattern and organisation "of work", *ie* between full-time and other categories.

The extent of Labour Flexibility

Comprehensive, national information on the extent of labour flexibility is not available. For functional, temporal and numerical flexibility limited research surveys have been published and can be supplemented by reports in newspapers and specialist publications. These are helpful but by their nature are rarely repeated and therefore date quickly. However it is still possible to paint a reasonably useful, impressionistic picture from what is in print.[6]

An exception to this is the fourth dimension. The Government has consistently maintained that the growth in 'flexible' jobs has more than compensated for the decline in permanent jobs. This policy interest is reflected in the 1981–85 Labour Force Survey published by the Department of Employment in 1987.[7] The 1985 picture is shown in Table 1.1.

TABLE 1.1
The Flexible Labour Force, 1985

Part-time workers	4.4 million
Self-employed	2.6 million
Temporary workers	1.3 million
Total	8.3 million

In 1985 the total figure of 8.3 million amounted to just over a third of those in employment, an increase of 16% from 1981, with temporary workers showing the fastest growth. Permanent workers, in contrast, fell by 6% over the same period.

This picture was confirmed by Catherine Hakim of the Department of Employment in her detailed study of the flexible labour force cited earlier. Her work also stressed the analytical importance of recognising the overlap between the three categories (*ie* some workers had jobs which combined two or even three of temporary, part-time and self-employed) and that whilst roughly one third of all employment was flexible, there were wide variations between industries — *eg* from 6% in energy and water supply to 60% in agriculture — but with the heaviest concentration, in terms of numbers, in the service sector, *ie* hotels and catering, distribution, repairs, and professional and business services. Institute of Manpower estimates have emphasised the importance of the seven

fastest growing sectors for temporary employment, overlapping
with Hakim's list — hotels, catering, wholesale distribution, retail
distribution, banking, building societies and insurance.[8] The IMS
estimates also show the greatest geographical concentrations in the
South East of England, East Anglia and South West England,
suggesting the connection between high rates of economic growth
and demand for flexible labour.

Studies and surveys reporting the other dimensions do suggest
that they are widespread but are cautious as to the *depth* of flexible
labour innovations. Thus the 1985 IMS study for NEDO concludes:

> "Although the observed changes were widespread, they did
> not cut very deeply in most of the firms, and therefore the
> outcome was likely to be marginal, ad hoc and tentative,
> rather than a purposeful and strategic thrust to achieve
> flexibility. Short-term cost saving, rather than long-term
> development, dominated management thinking, save where
> substantial new investment was involved. As a result, we
> noted rather greater management interest, particularly in the
> service sector, in deploying cheap 'peripheral' labour, rather
> than changing the employment culture at the 'core'"[9]

The conclusions of the employer-oriented IMS study have
been confirmed by the Labour Research Department's recent
and detailed survey of local trade unionists and full-time
officials. This monitored change since 1981 and concluded that
the promotion of flexible working practices by Government
and employers was motivated by cost-cutting and reductions
in the permanent labour force. At the same time the promotion by employers of the concept of the flexible firm was
". . . creating a false impression of radical change . . ."[10]

Some recent notable examples from different industries are:

- *Shipbuilding*: Agreements at John Brown's on the Clyde (1986)
  and at Smith's Dockyard on the Tees (1987) reduced grades and
  partly eliminated job demarcations.
- *Cars*: Nissan's agreement at its Washington plant with the AEU
  (1987) to introduce temporary labour on the assembly line at
  peak periods.
- *Chemicals and Oil*: Shell Stanlow's three year deal (1987)
  continuing earlier flexibility provisions on shiftworking reductions in the numbers of grades and maintenance tasks for
  process workers.
- *Coal*: British Coal is progressively introducing flexible shift

patterns at a number of existing pits in Nottinghamshire and new pits at Hawkhurst Moor in Coventry, Asfordby in Leicestershire and Margam in South Wales. The Welsh pit now recognises the Union of Democratic Miners which accepts the principle of flexible working within a six day week.

● *Engineering*: The present selective strikes by the CSEU are the latest round in a long-running dispute with the EEF which seeks an extension of flexible working in its member companies in return for a reduction in the nationally-set working week.

Conclusions: The significance of Labour Flexibility

Labour flexibility is not, in its totality, wholly opposed by workers and trade unions. For example, a TUC study[11] citing Shell Carrington's agreements whilst pointing to the problem of job insecurity even among "core" workers, does discuss the potential advantages of functional flexibility — *ie* making jobs more interesting and increasing responsibility for output and quality. Multi-skilling can of course increase workers' marketable skills as well as job interest and responsibility, especially if allied to new technology. But such innovations need not be a fixed-sum game in which highly-skilled workers maximise pay, security and benefits at the expense of their less-skilled brothers and sisters pushed into "peripheral" and down-graded tasks, while others are offered redundancy in the context of the worst employment prospects for a generation.

Superficially, numerical and temporal flexibility have clear advantages for employers measured in terms of labour cost minimisation and control of the workforce, especially where market demand has natural seasonal or cyclical patterns. For workers on the permanent payroll there is the much stressed benefit of a reduced working week. But this is an average arrangement with sometimes very wide variations. For example, a recent agreement between Ever Ready, the TGWU and ASTMS provided for a working week ranging from $25\frac{1}{2}$ to 45 hours around a cut in the average working week from 39 to 36 hours. The "annualised hours" approach also featured in Blue Circle's 1987 deal and an Industrial Society Survey claims that 500,000 workers are now covered by such agreements.

These working patterns are a major extension of the "continental rota" and "flexible rostering" responses to technical and social imperatives in industries such as steel, hospitals, transport and leisure. The case for their general extension may even be suspect on economic grounds given their implications for workers' productivity and their health and safety, apart from the disruptive effects on leisure and social life which are already well understood with regard to conventional double and three shift working.

The response of the trade unions to flexible labour proposals and agreements is inevitably pragmatic and strongly influenced by their current weakness. The T&GWU in particular "accepts" the rapid growth in temporary work, but is campaigning to recruit these workers into membership and to negotiate rights equal to those of permanent workers in all future agreements. But such a stance is clearly *faute de mieux* and is dictated by high unemployment and massive losses of members. Nor are begetters of the flexible firm entirely sanguine about the continuing health of their offspring.

> "Is it wise to go on using the fear of unemployment as a major lubricant for achieving flexibility? Continuing high levels of unemployment mean that it is possible to go on this way for some time, but if we are to secure permanent change in our employment culture then we need to consider shifting to more durable 'carrots', designed to secure compliance out of mutual commitment and shared goals rather than the cold comfort of market forces."[12]

PROFESSOR BRIAN TOWERS
University of Strathclyde

References

1 Ronald Dore, *Flexible Rigidities: Industrial Policy and Structural Adjustment in the Japanese Economy*; Athlone Press: 1986.
2 Michael Cross, *Contracting-out in UK Manufacturing Industry: Recent Development and Issues*, City University Business School: 1989.
3 For historical and evalutive accounts, see Robert B McKersie, and Laurence C Hunter, *Pay, Productivity and Collective Bargaining*, Macmillan: 1973 and B Towers, et al, *Bargaining for Change*, Allen and Unwin: 1972
4 NBPI, *Hours of Work, Overtime and Shiftworking*, Report No 161, Cmnd 4554, HMSO: December 1970, plus Supplement Cmnd 4554–1
5 A recent study even suggests that it perhaps never was inferior. See Theo Nichols, *The British Worker Question: a new look at workers and productivity in manufacturing*, Routledge & Kegan Paul: 1986
6 A short selection is Catherine Hakim, 'Trends in the flexible workforce', *Employment Gazette*: November 1987, pp 549–560; John Atkinson, and N Meager, 'Is flexibility just a flash in the pan?',

Personnel Management: September 1986; 'Flexibility', Labour Research Department, *Bargaining Report* No 56: November 1986

7 Department of Employment, reported in *Financial Times*: 5 February 1987.

8 Amin Rajan and Richard Pearson, *UK Occupation and Employment Trends to 1990*, Butterworth: 1986.

9 Atkinson and Meager, op cit, p 26

10 Labour Research Department, op cit, p 6.

11 National Education Centre, TUC 1986

12 Atkinson and Meager, op cit p 29.

2
Workforce 2000: An Agenda for Action

People and jobs: the supply side

The UK workforce is undergoing a major change. The change is being brought about by demographic factors, with fewer young people entering the workforce in the years ahead.

The process has already begun. At the start of the 1980s, there were nearly 2.7 million people aged 16 to 19 years old in the civilian labour force in Great Britain. By 1989, this had fallen to 2.5 million. By 1994, the number is expected to fall below 2 million.

With the passage of time, this squeeze inevitably applies up the age range. In 1987, there were nearly 3.7 million people aged 20 to 24 in the civilian labour force. By 1994, the number is expected to be below 3.2 million, with further decline in later years.

We have some 7.8 million people aged 16 to 24. By the year 2000, we are projected to have just over 6.1 million. The rise in numbers thereafter is expected to be limited and shortlived. This decline in numbers of young people is even more remarkable when set against the backdrop of a growing total population, with more and more older people.

The figures show a long term, substantial contraction in the number of potential new entrants to the labour market, with the likelihood that the squeeze will become still more intense as more young people remain in education.

A shrinking UK workforce?

What will be the impact on the UK workforce as a whole of this decline in the number of young labour force entrants? It would be easy to jump to the assumption that, if fewer young people join the workforce, then the workforce must shrink.

But in practice, that is not the trend forecast. The size of the total civilian labour force in Great Britain climbed from 26.2

million in 1980 to 27.9 million by 1989, a rise of 6.5%. In the coming decade, the pace of increase is expected to slacken, but nonetheless continued growth in the workforce is projected. By the year 2000, the total civilian labour force is expected to number 28.6 million, 2.5% above today's levels.

What explains this projected increase in the workforce, when fewer young people will be entering the labour market? The decline in the number of new labour market entrants coincides broadly with a decline in the number of people reaching retirement age. Far more importantly, the figures assume that an increasing proportion of women of working age will want to take paid employment.

In 1980, there were 10.6 million women in the civilian labour force, accounting for 40.3% of the workforce. By 1989, this had risen to 12 million, equal to 42.9%. By the year 2000, the number of women in the workforce is projected to reach 12.7 million, 44.4% of the total. Overwhelmingly, this projected increase in female employment is expected to come about as a result of more women returning to work more speedily after having children.

So, on existing projections, the decline in the number of young people entering the labour market will not reduce the size of the UK workforce in its composition.

What sort of a workforce?

The skills and abilities of the future UK workforce will be at least as important as its size.

The track record of the UK to date in terms of education and skill levels has been less than satisfactory. While the extent of skill shortages has fluctuated over the years, it has long been a constraint on parts of British business, as Chart 8 indicates. There are other measures, too, of the difficulties. In a CBI survey of private sector employers in 1986, 21.5% reported persistent shortages of certain skills. By 1989, this had risen to 36.4%. In 1986, some 54.7% of private sector employers reported difficulties in recruiting specific types of skilled employees. This figure had climbed to 70.8% by 1989. When asked about the general quality of job applicants, the results again indicated deterioration rather than improvement.

People and jobs: the demand side

We cannot assess how important changes in the future size and composition of the workforce will be for employers without looking at the numbers and types of jobs they are likely to be needing to fill.

Making accurate forecasts about future employment is notoriously difficult. At the start of the 1980s, for example, there were those who took the view that the numbers of people in employment was entering a permanent decline as a result of technological change. Such forecasts have a very long history indeed, appearing regularly over the years at times when unemployment has risen.

The figures, however, tell a very different story. Over the years, the long-term trend has been towards ever more people in employment and an ever higher proportion of people opting to work. The number of people who are economically active has shown a fairly steady expansion over the course of this century. In 1901, just over 16 million people were economically active. By 1951, the figure had climbed to 22.6 million. By 1989, the working population stood at 28 million. At the same time, a steadily increasing proportion of people have chosen to enter the job market. While in 1921 only 58% of the population were economically active, by 1961 this had risen to 60.5% and by 1989 to 62.8%.

There have been major changes in the structure and composition of UK employment as a result of changes in markets, technologies, products and processes. But across the economy as a whole, more and more jobs have been created over the years, far outnumbering those that have been lost.

One of the biggest changes in the structure of UK employment has been the decline in manufacturing jobs and the expansion of the services sector. In the early 1960s, fewer than one in every two British employees had a job in the services sector. By the late 1980s more than two out of three employers work in the services sector. What has occurred in recent decades has been a steady and large scale transfer of jobs from the manufacturing to the services sector.

What should we conclude abut the likely future demand for labour from this short review of past trends? First, despite periodic fears that technological change would destroy the need to employ people, what we have seen has been a fairly steady growth in jobs over many years. Second, while the numbers of jobs in manufacturing in the UK has declined steadily over the years, there is nothing inevitable about the pace of that decline or, indeed, about there being a decline at all.

It is of course, always dangerous to extrapolate past trends on into the future. Although total employment may have risen steadily during the course of this century, what evidence is there that the number of jobs will continue to increase in the years ahead? In the remainder of this section, we seek to answer two key questions.

The prospects for employment growth

In 1985, the CBI conducted a survey among a cross section of member firms to assess employer's views on future employment levels. The results indicated that, among all sizes of firms except the very largest, far more companies expected to increase their numbers of employees over the next five years than expected to reduce their workforces. . . .

The Institute for Employment Research at Warwick University is projecting an aggregate increase in UK employment of 1¾ million between 1987 and 1995.

The structure of employment has changed rapidly in recent years. In addition to the shift from manufacturing to service sector employment, there has been a rapid expansion in part-time and temporary employment. The number of part-time employees has climbed steadily, rising from 3.3 million in 1971 (15% of all employees) to nearly 5.4 million by 1988 (24% of all employees). The scale of the increase is shown in Chart 10. Temporary employment, too, has grown rapidly in recent years, accounting for nearly 6% of the workforce by 1988.

The rapid growth of both of these types of employment was anticipated by employers taking part in the CBI's 1985 survey. In all, 27% of employers at that time expected the proportion of part-timers in their workforces to increase over the next five years, while only 14% expected a decrease. The proportion of employers expecting an increase in part-timers exceeded the proportion expecting a decrease in all sizes of companies, with growth particularly expected by larger firms.

Our 1989 survey found even more positive expectations about the growth in part-time employment over the next five years. Of the employers surveyed, no less than 44% expect that the proportion of part-timers in their workforces will increase over the next five years. Only 5% anticipate a reduction in the proportion of part-timers. Once again, firms of all sizes expect to see growth in part-time jobs.

The Institute for Employment Research, too, anticipates continued rapid expansion in part-time jobs. Of the 1¾ million additional jobs it expects to see created in the period up to 1995, some two thirds are expected to be in the form of part-time jobs.

Like the growth in part-time working, the expansion in temporary employment was foreseen by employers participating in the CBI's 1985 survey. At that time, 27% of employers expected to increase the proportion of temporary workers they employed over the coming five years, against 14% expecting a decrease. Increases in temporary jobs were particularly anticipated by larger firms.

According to the 1989 survey results, this trend will be accelerated in the years ahead. Over the next five years, some 29% of companies expect to increase the proportion of temporary employees in their workforces. Only 10% foresee a decrease.

So, in the years ahead, the number of employers expecting to increase the size of their workforces greatly outnumber the number expecting to shed labour. At the same time, far more firms expect to increase part-time and temporary jobs than expect to reduce them. In summary, our projections point to more jobs, with more of them part-time and more of them temporary.

What else do available forecasts suggest about the nature of these new jobs? We have already noted that the growth in jobs is expected to be in the services and construction sectors, while continued slow decline is likely in manufacturing. In terms of occupations, the fastest growth is expected to be in professional and technical jobs. Growth to a somewhat lesser extent is also expected in many other occupations, including managerial occupations and in craft and skilled manual jobs. Indeed, only in the least skilled blue collar occupations are there expected to be reductions in numbers of jobs. In brief, the likelihood is that employers in the years ahead will want more people with more skills.

For employers, the main implications of the trends are clear. They point to increasingly intense competition among employers in the labour market. It will simply not be possible for employers as a whole to take on young employees in the numbers that we have seen in recent years. With more jobs to fill, requiring more skills, and with fewer new labour market entrants, there is a risk that pay levels may be driven up faster than is justified by improvements in performance, so raising unit labour costs and damaging our competitiveness. There are already signs that employers in some instances are responding to the fall in the numbers of young people by raising pay levels substantially.

What steps can be taken to minimise the potential problems? First and most obviously, employers will be considering ever more carefully the ways in which they use people. Employees are already a valuable, costly resource and they are likely to become still more so.

Employers will be looking to maximise the contribution from their existing workforces. Of course, much is already being done. Recent years have seen tremendous changes in such areas as improving the motivation of employees, enhancing skill levels and adapting work patterns to fit more closely the needs of employer and employees. More will be needed in the future if firms are to improve their retention of employees and to maximise their contribution.

Employers will be looking at where they use people. There are already great variations between different parts of the country in terms of the tightness of labour markets. Many employers in recent years have moved operations from one location to another to ease recruitment and retention difficulties. Given the considerable differences in demographic trends between different regions, such factors are likely to become still more important. Moreover, in at least some jobs, technology is opening the way for work to be done away from the company's main operations, perhaps through "telecommuting".

Employers will be seeking ways to enhance the size and skill levels of the "pool" from which they will be drawing recruits in the years ahead. Of course, there will still be large numbers of young people entering the workforce in the years ahead and it is important that their educational standards should be as high as possible.

Women in the UK already play a major role in the world of work. Latest figures show that a total of 11.6 million women aged over 16 were economically active in Great Britain in 1988 and that 42.7% of all employees were women. This trend is set to become still more pronounced in the years ahead — our survey of employers found over 32% intending to attract back more women who have left them to have children and over 38% planning to increase their recruitment of women.

While the European participation rates indicate that women's involvement in the labour market is comparatively high in this country, this mainly reflects the high level of part-time working amongst women in the UK. The UK has the highest level of part-time jobs as a percentage of all women working across the European Community, with 45% of female employees working part-time in the UK.

Of course, there are good reasons why so many women work part-time. The availability of part-time hours is often a determining factor behind whether a woman feels she can take up paid employment at all. However, the problems often associated with expanding part-time hours into high grade positions have the effect of confining many women to relatively junior and lower skilled jobs than they are capable of undertaking.

Nearly two-thirds of the women currently outside the labour market, questioned by Gallup in the survey of women and work said that they were interested in taking paid employment. With so many women wanting to work, why is there such a differential pattern of participation between men and women?

It can be difficult for a woman who has been away from work to care for children to find a job with hours that fit in with the time she wishes to spend with her children.

The Gallup survey of women and work showed that the most frequently cited factor in making a job attractive to a woman returner was the convenience of working hours. In all, 98% of the women in the survey cited this as either very or quite important in making a job attractive to them. When those women in the survey who were interested in returning to work were asked on what basis they would prefer to return to work, 43% said that they would like to return to part-time work, and 40% reported that they would prefer to return to work on a term-time only basis.

While the availability of part-time work is increasing, it tends to be located in a range of sectors such as retailing and services and is often restricted to fairly low level work.

There are a number of options that companies can consider in introducing more "hours to suit", ranging from an extension of part-time opportunities through term-time working, to working on a "temporary" basis. In addition to making more work available on more flexible bases, employers will want to consider ways of ensuring that flexible working hours do not have the effect of confining women to low level occupations.

Temporary working: Some women may not wish to enter a permanent contract of employment with an employer but may welcome the opportunity of working on a temporary basis.

Working for a temporary employment agency is often an attractive way to return to the workplace, and employment agencies can be used to provide skilled staff to companies. (See *Manpower*, p. 81.)

Companies can also maintain registers of women, perhaps former employees who have left to have children, who can be contacted from time to time, to see if they could work for short periods. Such schemes may be especially useful for staffing during particularly busy periods. In addition, they provide an opportunity for companies to keep in touch with staff, who might, at a later date, be willing to consider joining the company on a permanent basis.

The Over 50s: a neglected resource

The Over 50s age group is currently less active in the labour market than other age groups. In 1987, the latest date for which figures are available, 74% of this group was economically active, compared with 90.1% for people aged 16–49. Those over 50s within five years of pension age have the lowest activity rate of any group of working age, with only just over half economically active. Our survey results, however, show employers planning to reverse this trend, with more than 38% intending to increase their recruitment of older people.

Employment characteristics of the Over 50s

Older workers tend to be less occupationally mobile than younger age groups. At any particular time, only about 2% of the over 50s who are in jobs are looking for new or additional jobs. This is likely to reflect the fact that older workers are likely to be in a job that they are happy in, and possibly their desire to protect pension entitlements. Older workers are also much more likely to remain in the same occupation or professional class. In the age group 55 and above, there is virtually no movement from one year to the next. More than 96% are still with the same employer in the same occupation 12 months later. Older workers tend to be less likely to make job related geographical moves than younger people. With fewer years to work before retirement, the benefits to the employee and the employer are likely to be outweighed by the costs and disruption involved.

The proportion of older workers working part-time is somewhat greater than other age groups, particularly in the five years before State pension age. As would be expected, the majority of part-timers over 50 are female, although around 7% of 60 to 65 year old males are in part-time employment.

Making better use of older employees: options for employers

It is undoubtedly the case that age is used as a way of filtering job applications. Age limits are usually regarded as guidelines and employers often go beyond the specified age limit at least occasionally, in order to find the right candidate. Around 80% of personnel directors and recruiters agreed with the proposition that "too many executive job ads impose needless age restrictions."

There are signs that attitudes towards older people are changing. Those employers who want to take on older workers are likely to follow the pattern set by companies such as B & Q and Tesco, and advertise specifically for older people.

Taking account of older worker's views

The CBI Gallup Poll showed that 69% of retired over 50s who wished to return to work would prefer to work on a part-time basis. Many wished to undertake some combination of paid work, leisure activities and voluntary work.

Despite the fact that most people miss the money associated with work, a good level of pay is not the most important consideration in the minds of those who would consider returning to work. Interesting and varied work, a friendly and supportive atmosphere, opportunities to use their abilities, and an easy journey to work, are all judged to be more important, and convenient working hours are only marginally less important.

Re-employing the Unemployed

Despite the very rapid rise in employment since the early 1980s, there continue to be large numbers of unemployed people. The numbers are much greater in some regions than in others, but across the UK as a whole there are hundreds of thousands of people who have been out of work for lengthy periods. They represent an important resource which should not be neglected, quite apart from the human and social costs which unemployment imposes.

There are a variety of reasons why the long term unemployed have difficulty in finding new jobs. These can include geographical and occupational immobility, poor health, or disabilities, and the "unemployment trap" caused by the interaction of the tax and social security systems.

People who have been out of work for a long time often lack the occupational skills required for many jobs in today's labour market. Many of the new jobs require very different types of skills and qualifications. Moreover, the growth of new employment has taken place most rapidly in the South and East Anglia, rather than the regions which experienced major job losses from the recession. The longer people remain out of work, the harder it is for them to re-enter the workforce, as they lose the habit of working, their confidence and their occupational skills.

Options for Employers

The long term unemployed do experience particular problems in taking up full-time work. Employers usually prefer to take their new employees from those already employed, or to employ those who have only been unemployed for a short period. It is a common prejudice that the skills and the work commitment of the individuals who have been out of work for a year or more will have atrophied. Employers will want to examine their methods of recruitment and selection to check whether they are perhaps unreasonably ruling out or discouraging applications from long term unemployed. They may also want to consider the scope of using Employment Training as a means of bringing skills and work habits of the unemployed up to standard, although the scheme has not been without its critics. But it has to be acknowledged that a major role in preparing the long term unemployed for re-entry into work and for lifting the obstacles they face, lies with the Government.

AGENDA FOR ACTION

Demographic change demands an effective response on the part of businesses and Government alike. Employment policies respond to the increasing need to recruit and retain from different groups of the adult population. Attention will need to be focused on the employment of women, older people, ethnic minority groups and the unemployed. In addition, companies may seek to increase their recruitment of non-UK nationals. The preceding sections have shown the range of options open to companies and the actions that should be considered by the Government to enable employers to adapt successfully to demographic change. Some of the main points to emerge are set out below.

OPTIONS FOR COMPANIES

ACTION FOR GOVERNMENT

Women: the workforce of the future?

Enhancing maternity provisions, offering career breaks and providing greater support to women returning from maternity leave can improve a company's ability to retain female employees.

While the issues are complex, consideration needs to be given to the principles and the practical impact of current policies regarding the taxation of employer subsidies to child care.

OPTIONS FOR COMPANIES

ACTION FOR GOVERNMENT

A wide range of options are open to the company considering providing assistance with child care. Whatever the option adopted, involvement with child care can be a decisive factor in whether and how quickly a woman returns to work after maternity leave, as well as being a powerful tool in recruitment.

Both central and local Government must play a part in providing and supporting high quality child care for pre-school and school age children.

Introducing more flexible and part-time working arrangements can enable a company to benefit from the pool of women who are not available for work on a full-time basis. Thought can also be given to moving such work arrangements into managerial positions.

Training and retraining opportunities can be made available to women returners both to update skills and to enable women to move into new areas of work.

The Over 50s: a neglected resource?

Consideration needs to be given to minimising the use of age restrictions in recruitment and selection. By imposing unnecessary age limits, employers are denying themselves access to a valuable source of talented and committed employees.

The abolition of the Pensioner's Earnings Rule will be of considerable benefit to companies seeking to employ people beyond state retirement age. However, the need for greater flexibility in state pensions remains.

The introduction of more flexible working arrangements is important if companies are to retain and recruit older employees. Many people may only want to work part-time towards the end of their careers.

The CBI therefore believes that the Government should introduce a flexible decade of retirement around a common pension age of 65.

OPTIONS FOR COMPANIES
ACTION FOR GOVERNMENT

Consideration can be given to new ways of using the experience of older people. For example, retirees may be able to undertake particular tasks on a "consultancy" or "temporary" basis.

Employment and the ethnic minorities

In addition to the thorough and effective promotion of equal opportunities, companies can increase their recruitment of people from ethnic minority groups via greater outreach and promotion.

Re-employing the unemployed

Attention needs to be focused on recruitment and selection methods to ensure that companies are not unreasonably ruling out applications from the long-term unemployed.

Greater attention needs to be paid to ensuring that the Social Security system provides incentives rather than disincentives for the unemployed to take up paid employment, for example, through enhanced earnings disregards. The operation of the Social Security System can have a particularly adverse impact on the ability of single parents to take up paid work.

Although the scheme is not without critics, involvement with Employment Training can increase a company's ability to recruit from the long-term unemployed.

Proper resourcing must be given to, and positive use made of, programmes aimed at fostering greater confidence and awareness of opportunities among the unemployed.

Confederation of British Industry

3
Sub-Contracting: A TUC View

Introduction

The TUC would like first to welcome the Church of Scotland initiative to widen the debate about the changing nature of employment and the opportunity given to present a trade union perspective on the topical and controversial issue of sub-contracting.

This article begins by looking at the construction industry where the use of subcontractors is widespread. In particular, focusing on the use of "labour-only sub-contracting", which has been a source of considerable concern to the TUC and unions. The safety of construction workers and the quality of workmanship forms the basis of the trade union movement's opposition to "labour-only sub-contractors".

The issues surrounding contracting out and compulsory competitive tendering in the public sector are explored in the second part of the article. The so-called "Three Es" — Economy, Effectiveness and Efficiency — underlying the Government's pursuit of the privatisation of services in the NHS and local government are challenged and found to be wanting.

The final section of the article finds that the significance of the increased use of sub-contracting in the economy as a whole has been exaggerated by many commentators. In addition, a question mark is placed over the assumption that this trend will continue into the 1990s as firms become more and more concerned with quality rather than cost reduction.

But what is sub-contracting? It is simply when an organisation (public or private) essentially hires another firm to provide a service or good, or undertake a particular activity, on its behalf. This may involve a sub-contractor providing specialist knowledge and skills that the organisation does not readily possess, or it may entail contracting out of an activity previously carried out in-house. Not all sub-contracting is "bad" from a trade union point of view, but neither is all of it "good".

Sub-contracting in Construction

There is a good deal of terminology used when discussing the role of sub-contracting in the construction industry and this needs to be clarified. It is common to hear main contractors (or their managers) speak about "the employer". In this context "the employer" is the person — or more usually a public or private body — that has ordered building works. But "the employer" in this sense is perhaps more easily identified (by those inside and outside the industry) as the client or customer. In addition, it is important to make clear distinctions between different forms of sub-contracting in the construction industry.

The construction industry in most countries, the UK included, embraces many types of sub-contractors. This is traditional and perhaps as it should be. More precisely, these firms are often specialist sub-contractors. In a building contract, such firms could be responsible solely for plumbing; for electrical wiring; for glazing; for internal woodwork; or for putting in place external cladding. The list of such specialist tasks is not endless but, in the construction industry of today, it has been considerably lengthened by the changing nature of work in the industry and the growing sophistication of many buildings, particularly those for industrial or commercial use.

This has led to the introduction of practices such as management contracting. Under this system, a leading household name contractor undertakes to provide a building for a client but, apart for a few leading site managers, there is unlikely to be any building operatives employed by the main contractor on site: instead, all the work is separated into discrete parcels and given to sub-contractors with the main contractor acting more as co-ordinator than as a traditional main contractor engaged in at least some of the building work directly.

But, reference to sub-contractors in the construction industry is often not in relation to those firms providing specialist skills, but to *"labour-only sub-contractors"*. This is a very different matter and one that has attracted considerable trade union opposition since its emergence on a large scale in the "Barber boom" of the early 1970s. This aspect of sub-contracting in the construction industry is often referred to as "the lump". Typically, building operatives will be on site — to all visible intents and purposes appearing to be employees — but instead they will be either individually self-employed or self-employed and part of a gang. Direct employment has continued to decline as a proportion of total employment in the construction industry. Self-employment has grown by 53% since 1981 and is forecast to reach 40% of total employment in construction by 1995.

The system of "labour-only sub-contracting" in the construction industry has been opposed by unions and the TUC on a number of grounds:

- In terms of the *pay and conditions of workers* employed in the industry. The growth of "labour-only sub-contracting" is a major destabilising force within the industry, particularly in relation to national collective bargaining agreements and therefore on the pay and conditions of directly employed workers. This is especially the case where both are employed side by side on a site, but are employed under different rates of pay and terms of employment. Self-employed workers are paid without tax deducted at source and employers are able to avoid National Insurance contribution costs, holiday stamp payments, pay for public holidays, and are able to sidestep many of the legal requirements imposed by the Employment Protection Act. In short, many of the benefits offered by the law and by trade union negotiation;
- *Health and safety in construction*: The incidence of major and fatal injuries in the construction industry has risen faster than in manufacturing, at least in part because of corner-cutting by "cowboy" contractors and the competitive pressures this then puts on other firms. Moreover, because of the lack of liability and employer and union guidance, labour-only sub-contractors are likely to be both more ignorant of, and less likely to comply with, health and safety regulations. Lack of safety awareness and unwillingness to comply with safety requirements on site can pose as big a danger to directly employed workers as it can the self-employed themselves;
- As well as health and safety, *training* has also suffered as a result of the growth of self-employment and labour-only sub-contracting by undermining the industry's training base. The result has not only been a fall in the number of apprenticeships on offer in the private sector, but also reductions in the numbers of training places offered by local authority Direct Labour Organisations (DLOs). Private contractors who employ more labour-only sub-contractors feel they have less commercial justification for maintaining training levels. In addition, many of these labour-only sub-contractors are not recognised by the Construction Industry Training Board (CITB) and therefore do not pay the training levy. CITB in 1985 itself concluded that " . . . the growth of self-employment could pose problems for the quality and

accessibility to the industry of skilled labour supply". The quality of workmanship within the industry will inevitably suffer as a result;

- *Tax avoidance:* The informal or "black" economy generally, but especially in construction, is aimed at avoiding taxation. The use of non-declared "cash in hand" payments to self-employed workers is common. To try and overcome these problems the Inland Revenue issues 714 certificates to workers with established and clean tax records allowing them, on production of the certificate, to claim self-employed status. Except for workers holding 714 certificates construction employers are obliged to deduct from earnings at the normal PAYE rate. Although there are many genuine self-employed tradesmen and women holding 714 certificates, there are substantial abuses of the 714 system, often practised in connivance with contractors.

As the sub-contracting chain lengthens, so does the scope for abuse. In order to reduce the problems associated with labour-only sub-contracting highlighted above, the TUC and unions have called for:

- The *construction regulations* to be amended to make controllers of sites (the main or the managing contractor) responsible for co-ordinating all health and safety matters in line with the recommendations of the independent Health and Safety Inspectorate;
- That more *health and safety inspectors* be made available for construction work;
- A *register of operatives* to be introduced, with statutory authority to ensure that only registered construction operatives are employed on construction work; and,
- A statutory *register of contractors and sub-contractors* (perhaps similar to that operating in Belgium). There would be a number of terms and conditions attached to the register. Clients using unregistered contractors or sub-contractors would then be liable for payments with respect to tax or employment obligations of the contractor to the state.

The CEGB was one of the first major employers to recognise the problems involved in the use of a chain of sub-contractors in the construction and engineering industry and now operates a set of rules for the effective planning and co-ordination of not only health and safety matters, but also of the work undertaken by sub-contractors in order to ensure high levels of workmanship and completion of building and engineering work on time.

The TUC, unions, and those concerned with the future of the industry, will continue to campaign for these policies aimed at achieving a construction industry characterised by good employment, excellent health and safety, and a reputation for good workmanship rather than poor.

Contracting-out in the Public Sector

The 1988 Local Government Act requires local authorities (LAs) in England, Scotland and Wales to put services out to tender. The services subject to competitive tendering being: refuse collection; cleaning; catering; maintenance, and repair, with more in the pipeline. The tendering regime is now in place (the deadline set out in the Act was April 1989) and all six services have to be put out to tender by April 1991, with parks and ground maintenance to be phased in over five years. The Act also bars LAs from stipulating conditions on tenders (*ie* contract compliance) relating to "non-commercial" matters, including terms and conditions of employment and the use of labour-only sub-contractors.

But the Government has had to make contracting-out of services compulsory in the 1988 Act because, as a voluntary option, public authorities, including Conservative controlled ones, have clearly rejected privatisation in favour of direct labour in-house provision, despite exultations by Government ministers of the benefit to be derived from contracting out. According to the pro-privatisation pressure group, the Public and Local Services Efficiency Campaign (PULSE), only 10% of Conservative councils by 1986 had responded to the Government's ideas.

So what are the arguments for contracting-out made by the Government and its supporters, and why, after seven years of propaganda, has the policy received so little support within the public sector that the Government has felt compelled to make "competitive tendering" compulsory by statute?

The arguments put forward by the Government and its pro-privatisation supporters in favour of contracting-out in the public sector are:

- The ability to test the effectiveness of an existing service against alternatives;
- The incentive which competition brings to the existing service to cut costs;

● Improvements in quality of service, because private contractors are prepared to invest in new equipment and methods of working to achieve savings and because the contractor knows that he will lose the contract if the customer is not satisfied.

These are the so-called "Three Es" — Effectiveness, Economy and Efficiency — which underlie the Government's policies on contracting out and compulsory competitive tendering.

The TUC opposes the Act on a number of grounds, not least that of local democracy and accountability. For example, the Act takes away the right of democratically accountable local authorities to subsidise school meals; and, by setting profit targets, undermines their ability to decide prices and public access in accordance to local circumstances and needs, for example, in relation to sports and leisure facilities. But in this paper, we shall concentrate on the "Three Es" argument used by the Government in support of contracting-out and compulsory competitive tendering.

Competitive tendering has had an adverse effect on levels of pay and conditions, on the employment prospects of disadvantaged groups, on the industrial relations climate among the remaining workforce, on staff morale and on management time. This is not surprising, as the major savings a contractor can make are in labour costs. Even where pay rates are higher, earnings are reduced because of limited overtime pay and the absence of bonus schemes. Conditions of service are nearly always worse, with poor sick-pay, little or no pension arrangements, and less holiday entitlement. Even where the in-house workforce has "successfully" bid, the unions and workforce have paid a high price in terms of loss of earnings, reduced employment, cuts in part-timers standard hours, and in holiday entitlement.

Yet despite the savings made in terms of labour costs, the overall level of savings made from contracting-out and competitive tendering have been small; no more than 10% on average compared to initial Government claims that savings in the order of 25% would be achieved by competitive tendering.

The costs to the NHS of administering competitive tendering are considerable given that a tender document can run to several hundred pages and take months to prepare. The National Union of Public Employees (NUPE) has estimated from its own research that the failure rate of private contractors is between 5 and 10%, *ie* the withdrawal of the contractor because of bankruptcy or inability to meet the requirements of the tender (not least because many contractors are inexperienced and unaware of the difficulties involved in providing a service) or simply as a result of poor performance. For example, one private contractor, Mediguard Services, forfeited £8,500 of its fees in penalties only two months after starting a contract at North Manchester General Hospital, because of its failure to clean operating theatres and toilets properly and for hiring untrained staff. The costs of contract termination (for whatever reason) are substantial, with the tender process having to begin once more. In addition, the cost of monitoring the performance of private contracts can often wipe out any initial savings made by contracting-out.

Moreover, any savings made through lower labour costs do not encompass the lower levels of service quality provided by private contractors — there is a reduction in the effectiveness of the service and the *value for money* achieved. The increased pressure of work means less time for training and proper health and safety practice. The lower wages and poor conditions of employment cause recruitment and retention difficulties with high staff turn-over contributing to deteriorating standards of service. Last June, Cambridge Evening News reported that "complaints about cleaning standards are still averaging more than 200 a week, with poor performance, staff shortages and high absenteeism a regular feature of health authority reports", a situation arising from the use of private cleaning contractors, such as OCS Hospital Services, which had no sick-pay scheme, no pension scheme, and pay their workers low wages.

In addition, *flexibility* is reduced because changes in provision in line with locally expressed needs requires renegotiation of the contract with the private contractor — a time-consuming and costly exercise.

Competitive tendering is unlikely to test the effectiveness of existing service when, in the contract, refuse and cleaning markets, just two companies (ADT and BET), hold around 60% of LA refuse collection and street cleaning contracts and a similar share of NHS cleaning contracts, and some 40 per cent of civil service cleaning contracts.

There is a tension between the so-called "Three Es" not recognised in the Government's arguments. Increased "Economy" does not necessarily lead to greater "Effectiveness" and "Efficiency". The experience of contracting-out in the NHS and local government over the last ten years suggests that greater economy (*ie* lower costs) has reduced the effectiveness and efficiency of service provision. A recent survey by the General and Municipal Boilermakers (GMB) union of local government contracts awarded in the first round of competitive tendering, found that almost 8 in 10 contracts have gone to in-house services, or Direct Service Organisations (DSOs). This suggests that in-house workforces are not wasteful of scarce public resources and do already provide an effective service.

The TUC and unions would welcome any initiative to genuinely improve the quality of service provision, but this is not achieved through the undermining of workers' jobs, pay, and conditions of service.

Instead, the effectiveness and efficiency of service provision in the public sector should be promoted through a *Quality Commission* which would disseminate 'best practice' and enhance service quality which reflects local circumstances and needs.

There is, of course, a social and moral aspect to this debate. The enforced tendering and contracting-out of services in the NHS and local government, predominately affects most severely those workers already at a disadvantage in the labour market. Research by the Institute of Personnel Management and Income Data Services Public sector Unit (1988) found that personnel managers in local government, and even more so in the NHS, saw contracting-out as distorting and disrupting policies, particularly equal opportunity policies, that had built up over many years and bearing particularly hard on the acknowledged low-wage earners within the workforce.

The TUC believes that a combination of commercial and social objectives embodied in contract compliance is not incompatible with efficient service provision. Far from it, as experience has shown: in fact, direct labour, employed at good rates of pay and conditions of service, is an essential prerequisite for flexible and high quality service provision.

Sub-contracting in the 1980s and 1990s

The level of sub-contracting has increased in the construction industry and in the public sector, but has it increased significantly across the whole of the economy? Not according to a recent survey by researchers based at Warwick University, who found that over 60% of companies reported no change in the level of sub-contracting over the previous five years. The increases reported by 37% were concentrated in those parts of the firms's operations, for example catering, cleaning and transport, where it has long been the practice to sub-contract (Pollert 1987). Examples of the sub-contracting of mainstream activities are comparatively rare (Marginson *et al*, 1988), not least because firms are able to maintain a standard of quality and security of supply in-house that is difficult to achieve through sub-contracting.

Moreover, some of the overall increase in sub-contracting and other forms of so-called "peripheral" employment (*ie* part-time, temporary and casual, and self-employment) is due to the shift from manufacturing (where it has always been relatively rare) towards the service sector where sub-contracting has always been more common.

A study examining the growth of sub-contracting in the 1980s also found that the use of sub-contracting had mainly been driven by a desire to cut costs, but "the extensive use of contractors has not yielded the cost or performance benefits sought" (Dr Michael Cross, 1989). In fact, it has been reported that there are some signs that sub-contracting, of maintenance services for example, is in decline because of the improved quality of in-house services (*Financial Times*, 7 December 1988).

The 1990s will see a growing emphasis on quality over cost and will seek to regain and maintain control over all aspects of production in order to compete in this more demanding environment. Of course, the sub-contracting of specialist labour, such as computer programmers for example, for particular "one-off" exercises is widely used by many organisations and is often the most appropriate policy and will continue.

Conclusion

The TUC and trade unions are not against sub-contracting — it can and does serve a useful purpose. But the trade union movement *is* against sub-contracting as a cynical exercise to undermine workers' rights, including trade union representation, and pay and conditions of employment. It is not acceptable to use sub-contracting as a means of evading the responsibilities of being an employer, whether in the public or private sectors.

In the construction industry, the use of "labour-only sub-contractors", if not properly and effectively regulated, actually increases the risks to workers' health and safety in an already potentially dangerous industry.

In the public sector the use of private sub-contractors to provide, for example, hospital cleaning services in the NHS, not only results in lower wages and conditions of employment, but also affects the quality of health care that is available to the people of the United Kingdom.

The effect that sub-contracting of this kind can have on quality of service or product will increasingly be felt, not only within the public sector, but in the private sector as well. As the 1990s approach more and more firms will be seeking to maintain and re-establish control over quality from their sub-contractors and perhaps the debate will turn around.

I BRINKLEY
Trade Union Congress

4
An STUC View of the Labour Market

The changing Labour Market

While in the past seven years attention in the UK, including
Scotland, has focused on unemployment, another — perhaps just
as significant — aspect of the labour market has been somewhat
neglected. This concerns the profound changes in the nature and
quality of work and conditions of employment. Combined with
Government legislation, they have substantially tilted the balance
of power in favour of employers and against the unions. The
changes involve, among others:

- Skills — deskilling for the majority, upgrading for a minority.
  This is partly due to technological advance but also the shift
  from manufacturing to service industries;
- Job Security — the spread of casual, contract and part-time
  working;
- An accompanying removal of all or part of employment protection and social security provisions from those workers involved
  in the new conditions of work, leading to
- The emergence of two nations in the working community, with a
  widening gap between those in full-time, reasonably paid and
  relatively safe jobs and the increasingly disadvantaged rest.

The trend shows clearly a rising proportion of female labour in
Scotland, especially of part-timers, in an otherwise contracting
labour force. The share of part-timers in the female labour force
rose from 35% to 45% in just a decade, between 1975 and 1985, as
service industries grew and manufacturing shrank.

Part-time working

It is important here to distinguish between those who *choose* part-
time work and those who are presented with no other option. For

many women, the existing reality of social relations in our society
— and in particular the role of "carers" which falls overwhelmingly on the shoulders of women — continues to mean that part-
time work is a welcome option providing some economic
independence.

On the other hand, many women wish to have full-time jobs,
but have been denied this opportunity. In retailing, for example,
hours are overwhelmingly determined by "the needs of the
business" and not by the domestic responsibilities of the employee.
Again, young people are not "choosing" to work part-time, but
are having it thrust upon them as an alternative to the dole.

A recent SDA Survey on the Skills Pattern of the Information
Systems Industry in Scotland shows that of operators, clerks and
secretaries (which form almost half of the total labour force) 58%
are women. On the other hand, of the scientists, technologists and
technicians (nearly a quarter of the labour force) only 5% are
women. The conditions under which part-timers work are usually
inferior to the rest of the labour market.

A high proportion are employed in the lowest grade occupations,
low paid and often segregated from full-time fellow workers. A
recent study by the Banking, Insurance and Finance Union found
that part-timers are "overwhelmingly in the lowest paid, lowest
status jobs, without equal career opportunity". It claims that
Banks are employing part-timers increasingly to reduce full-time
staffs. One aspect of part-time working is the loss of Social
Security provisions. The first study found that up to 70% of the
part-timers worked 16 hours or less per week — the cut off point
for Social Security benefits.

The "Dual Labour Market"

Particularly worrying is the emergence of a clear division between
two classes of labour — "two nations" mentioned above — with
the smaller group of "core workers" and the easily disposable
"peripherals", leading to what has been described as a "dual
labour market"

The Institute of Manpower Studies at Sussex University des-
cribes a "new style company" of permanent career employees with
skills specific to the company, highly flexible and capable of being
retrained; the next group with more general skills and less job
security; the third group consisting of part-timers, job-sharers,
short-term contract staff and public subsidy trainees (presumably
YTS, etc.) with no job security whatever; and finally "external

staff" ranging from highly skilled fixed contract people to non-skilled such as office cleaners, canteen staff, etc. The last three groups are the "peripherals". It is no wonder that the present Government is enthusiastic about this development; and so are the employers, no longer having to bother about protective legislation which provides such benefits as severance pay, sick pay, holidays and pensions.

It is clear that temporary contract working is preferred only by those few who have highly transferable, and highly marketable skills (such as some systems analysists and some professional footballers) or who can exploit short-term tax advantages through the acquisition of technically self employed status (as in the case of labour only sub-contractors in the construction industry — the "Lump").

Other Labour Market changes

Three other developments in the labour market are well worth noting and taking into account. Firstly, there is the huge rise in youth unemployment which began in the mid 70s and accelerated sharply in the 1980s. The scale of the problem is illustrated by the statistics for under 25s (from 83,837 in January 1980 to 146,209 in January 1986) and school leavers in Scotland (up from 13,300 in 1980 to 20,130 in January 1987), leaving aside those on YTS and other special schemes.

Secondly, there is the differential rate in unemployment for blacks and whites. In Britain in 1983, the unemployment rates for whites was 11%: for those of West Indian origin it was 23.2%, and for those from the Indian sub continent 21.7%. Ethnic minority organisations in Scotland testify that similar problems exist North of the Border, especially among young people. Thirdly, there is the rise in self employment from 1.84 million in Britain in 1977 to 2.53 million in 1985.

How then should people in Scotland cope with these changes — many of which have been thrust upon them unbidden?

Clearly the fight against unemployment — by getting people back to real jobs — is the main priority. But the quality of that work is of great importance. The best, surest way of securing good conditions of work is by being organised in the appropriate union. However, it must also be recognised that employment legislation is a vital factor.

The Scottish Assembly and the British Government should aim to abolish low pay and put an end to discrimination at work. (The establishment of a Ministry for Women will greatly assist in these aims.) Recognising that part-time and temporary employment are on the increase, legislation giving permanent rights to temporary workers and full-time rights to part-timers should be adopted. Legislation must be backed with an adequate inspectorate. Public bodies (and private firms) should also adopt a "contract compliance" strategy — *ie* refusing to place contracts with companies who do not conduct good employment practices.

We must recognise that there is a place for part-time and temporary employment in the economy. However, conditions of employment under which part-timers are engaged must as far as possible be pro-rata to full-time workers. Full employment rights must be extended to all part-time and temporary workers, regardless of length of service or hours worked. These workers should have full pension rights, and equal pay.

Trade Union response

The success of the trades unions in withstanding the ravages of the last few years and continuing to represent and defend workers indicates the desire and need of people to be organised in their social and working relations. A positive attitude to the role of the unions by Government and employers must be fostered. Trades Union legislation should not hinder the unions from adequately representing their members, nor interfere in their internal rules and procedures.

Whilst it is the Government's job to legislate, there are some things which the unions can do now. For example, the Transport and General Workers' Union is spending £100,000 initially on a campaign to recruit temporary workers, estimated to number 1.7 million in the UK. The four main objectives are: 1. Exposing abuse of temporary labour; 2. Collective bargaining for temporaries; 3. Legislation giving them the same rights as permanent staff; 4. A recruitment drive to pursue these rights.

Several unions have urged greatly strengthened safeguards and legislative protection in what is likely to be continuing flexibility in the labour market. In a general comment the TUC points out that

> "the drive for 'flexibility' by many firms, using what is thought of as the Japanese model, entails job insecurity through short-term contracts, greater use of sub-contracting and a general protection from risk by establishing various 'buffers' within the workforce. Risk and uncertainty stemming

from the changing economic environment is borne not so much by the firm or risk capital shareholders but by employees and suppliers.

"An individual structure based on insecurity rather than participation is clearly unacceptable and appropriates the benefits of technical development to a secure and privileged core thereby creating a two-tier economy."

In essence, the unions in Scotland — as elsewhere in Britain — urgently need to ensure that they are able to meet the needs of all sections of the labour-force. Among the steps which should be taken now are:

- Refining union structures and practices to make them acceptable to women, part-time and ethnic minority workers;
- Devising packages aimed specifically at recruiting and servicing temporary workers, and ensuring that full-time and key lay officials are properly trained in the implementation of such packages;
- Using modern campaigning and marketing techniques to publicise the virtues of collective bargaining and collective action (*ie* solidarity);
- Campaigning for legislation to provide secure employment rights for *all* workers;
- Negotiating and monitoring the implementation of equal opportunity policies in employment;
- Putting the maximum possible pressure on employers (whether in the public or private sector) to pursue a policy of "contract compliance" with their suppliers of goods and services, to ensure that these suppliers meet minimum standards in relation to trade union rights and general employment policy;
- Negotiating massively improved child care facilities in the community and (where appropriate) at the workplace;
- Ensuring that there is a genuine place in the Trade Union Movement for young people, including those on training schemes;
- Co-ordinating recruitment campaigns to maximise their impact and minimise duplication of effort.

These are minimum requirements if working people in Scotland are to be able to advance their interests on a collective basis through the unions. In reality, there is no other basis on which they will advance. There is, however, another major problem which needs to be tackled if we are to make progress: training and retraining.

Conclusions

The task facing us is a formidable one: it is to *civilise*, to *humanise* and to *bring under democratic control* the profound changes taking place in society, as part of the struggle for workers' rights in a civilised world. In order that the kind of measures referred to in this section can be implemented in the interests of the overwhelming majority of people in our society, we will have to ensure that its structures and activities take full account of the needs of all workers, whether they are full-time or part-time, permanent, temporary, or presently unemployed. It will also require that trade union organisation takes into account the importance of training and retraining, and that unions ensure that they have a major say in the formulation of employers' training strategies.

In addition to the provisions described above, there will have to be a reappraisal of the hours, weeks, and years of our working lives; of holidays, "sabbaticals" (including vocational ones already noted) and the age of retirement. This is the kind of debate currently left to the House of Lords. The Scottish Assembly could address these vital, everyday, human issues democratically, and legislate in accordance.

In the new, civilised and busy society envisaged throughout this document, there will be no unemployment. We will need to make best use of the talents which all our people possess. Here we have outlined a Training Strategy which will meet the requirements not only of the economy, or employers, but of the Scottish people themselves.

Scottish Trade Union Congress

5
Women Across Europe:
The Impact of 1992

The following pages contain the background notes on which Ms Christine Crawley. MEP, Chair of the European Parliament Women's Committee, based her speech to the TUC Conference on "Women Across Europe: The Impact of 1992", at Congress House, Great Russell Street, London, on Wednesday May 2nd 1990.

We express our thanks to Johanna Fawkes of the TUC and to Christine Crawley for their courtesy in enabling this item to be included here.

1992 AND ITS EFFECTS ON WOMEN

Research so far

Very little research has been done so far on the impact of the Single European Market and women.

It is important not to see the issue of 1992 and women in isolation but to consider it in the context of women's overall position in the labour market. An understanding of the current problems experienced by women in the economy is essential if one is to even begin to assess the effects of 1992 on women.

It is also important to recognise that the effect of the single market will not be the same across the Community. Different countries will be affected in different ways and issues raised by the Single Market will vary according to national economic considerations. For example, demographic change will affect some countries and regions more than others.

Situation of women in the Labour Market

- *Women are less likely to be economically active than men:* 1986 European Labour market survey showed that 79% of men in the 14–65 age group were economically active compared to only 49% of women (UK figures are 84% and 61% respectively — difference due to the much larger number of part-time workers in UK)

● *Women are more likely to be unemployed than men:* Across Europe, the unemployment rate in 1988 was 11.9% for women, compared with 7% for men. NB: Britain shows a lower rate of unemployment for women — this could partly be due to the way we count the figures but also the large number of part-time workers in the UK labour force.

● *Women are paid less on average than men:* Women are paid between 14 and 34% less than men across the community.

● *Women are concentrated in certain sectors of the economy:* 90% of women in West Germany work in 12 occupational sectors
   One third of Dutch women are found in 4 occupations — sales assistants, secretaries, nurses, administration.

   In the UK two occupational groups (clerical and related personal services *ie* catering, cleaning, hairdressing) account for 52% of all working women (full and part-time).

   Women are concentrated in service rather than production and are more likely to work part-time than men.

Women and work: some current issues

● *Demographic Change:* This is an employment issue which will have a major effect on women in the 1990s. Over the next few years the number of school leavers joining the labour market will decrease dramatically — the 'demographic time bomb'. This will affect most of the countries in the European Community although the problem will be more acute in some countries than in others. The effect of this demographic change is already being felt by many employers who are finding it increasingly difficult to attract and retain skilled workers.

   These labour market shortages offer women returners the opportunity to fill some of the gaps, to press for better employment conditions, better pay and proper support so that they can combine domestic and work responsibilities. Already some employers, local authorities and, to a very limited extent, government are looking at ways of facilitating the participation of women in the labour market. Conferences, articles and television and radio programmes on Women and Employment are becoming commonplace.

● *Growth in the service sector of the economy:* Over the past few years, as manufacturing industry has declined, there has been a corresponding growth in the service sector. The growth in the service sector has largely accounted for the increase in the number of women participating in the labour market. This growth is likely to continue in the 1990s and could be seen as an opportunity for women to continue to play a more important role in the world of work. However, the decline in manufacturing industry has led to an overall reduction in skilled employment. Service jobs (many of them seen as traditionally 'women's jobs') are often contracted out by companies and this trend will increase — such jobs are usually insecure, low paid and do not carry the benefits of full-time, secure employment *ie* pension rights, training access etc.

• *Combining work with other responsibilities:* Childcare and the difficulties experienced by women who are struggling to combine domestic and employment responsibilities are inevitably major themes in the present discussions. The European Parliament has done considerable work on childcare across Europe and there is a tremendous variation across the Community in the provision available both of pre-school care and care for children of school age. The United Kingdom fares particularly badly in such comparisons.

The difficulties experienced by lone parents are particularly acute. Lone parents have above-average needs for childcare because they often have to manage without the help of a partner. Surveys have shown that lone parents tend to rely more heavily on relatives than mothers in two-parent households. Lone parents are often disadvantaged when it comes to paying for childcare because their income is almost inevitably well below that of a two-parent household.

Effects of 1992 on women

It is the case that, in general, women start from a worse economic starting point when it comes to a question of assessing the effects of 1992. Much more work needs to be done to examine regional differences and to attempt to assess their effects on women workers.

Even in those industries where increased competition may lead to more job opportunities, the *quality* of the jobs created must be an issue for women. The evidence available would tend to suggest that the trend towards flexibility in the labour market (often seen as having particular advantages for women) may in fact lead to more insecure work. With increased labour market flexibility, the organisations of the future are likely to consist of a small core of well-paid permanent workers, a small core of highly-paid consultants and a peripheral casual workforce who are badly paid, have minimal employment protection and little or no access to training or career development. It is likely that women will form the majority of this particular group.

The limited research carried out by the European Commission so far would tend to support the view that women are particularly vulnerable to the implementation of the Single Market:

- The 9 sectors identified by the commission as being particularly sensitive to 1992 changes all have a higher percentage of women working in them (pharmaceuticals, confectionery, woollen and cotton goods, jewellery, photographic equipment, toys, shoes and textiles and clothing).
- Increased competition is likely to result in a reduced demand for jobs requiring few qualifications — *ie* women's jobs.
- Free movement of labour will be more likely to discriminate against women than men — there are likely to be more cultural difficulties for women when it comes to uprooting and moving around the community for work or training.
- The expansion in the service sector especially childcare and cleaning may be seen by some as an opportunity for women but will do nothing to break down the female employment 'ghettos'.

Action needed if the effects on women are to be tackled

- More information is needed on the reality of women's working lives and the regional differences affecting them.
- Further information is needed on how far women are currently able to access European training programmes *eg* Comett, Erasmus.
- The European Parliament's Directives on part-time working, parental leave and other actions to protect women workers should be implemented without delay as a protection against an expansion in this insecure sector of the economy. It is also essential that those aspects of the Social Charter which will benefit women are implemented.
- If this is to happen, it is essential for the Commission to acknowledge that in Community action on issues such as social security, childcare cannot be seen as purely 'social' and therefore the remit of national governments. These issues have a critical impact on the working lives of women and on their access into

and development at work. They are "employment issues" which will increasingly affect the European economy. Their harmonisation is no less important than the harmonisation of tariff barriers and should be the responsibility of the whole community and not of individual governments.

CHRISTINE CRAWLEY
European Parliament Women's Committee

6
Sub-Contracting:
Storing up Trouble?

Introduction

The excitement surrounding the seminal report[1] produced by the National Economic Development Council and the Institute of Manpower Studies in 1986, has led to rising concerns about the growth of a "peripheral" underclass within the employment context. These concerns have exercised the minds of trade unionists, politicians and others worried about the creation of a Britain divided into groups of "haves" and "have nots".

The concept for which the report is best remembered is perhaps its introduction of the "core and periphery model" of employment. "Core" employees are those at the centre of an organisation's labour resource, enjoying security of employment, relatively high wages and occupational benefits, and receiving the bulk of any investment in training. Periphery workers, on the other hand, have little, if any, tenure, receive lower wages and benefits and not a great deal of training. The "peripheral" employee is likely to be part-time, temporary or sub-contract.

To some, the peripheral model seems to give substance to fears that employers, including Government, will drive down wages by converting previously full-time jobs into part-time (in all senses), low status and highly volatile employment filled by unorganised, low paid and unskilled workers. How sustainable are these fears? Has there been such a move? What advantages and disadvantages might flow from the change?

Some of these issues will be addressed in this article. At the Institute of Personnel Management we believe that human resources professionals must make every effort to dispel any misconceptions that exist about "the flexible firm". To perpetuate the mythology stores up problems for the future.

How new is Sub-contracting?

The report being prepared by the Industrial Mission concerns chiefly the issue of sub-contracting. It must be said, in passing, that much of the analysis below, particularly that part dealing with possible long term problems, is equally as relevant to any debate about part-time and temporary working. In many respects, sub-contracting is just one third of a numerical flexibility troika; it is rare to find it existing in isolation to other approaches to matching labour supply in an organisation to product/service demand.

Certainly the *concept* of sub-contracting as a legitimate working pattern is hardly new. Some years ago, the futurologist Alvin Toffler wrote of a post-industrial world'where consumers, whether of products, services or labour, would prefer to rent them than buy them outright. This forecast is easily discernable in the growth of the rental sector, franchising, leasing *etc*. More recently Charles Handy[2] has pcinted to the emergence of the "contractual organisation", which means the growing tendency for organisations to contract out more and more of their activities, preferring to pay fees for services rather than wages.

Peters and Waterman[3] drew attention to "sticking to the knitting" as a mark of the successful organisation; a view echoed in the NEDC/ IMS report which noted that companies (and public sector bodies even if by Government direction) were identifying those activities that were peripheral and could be sub-contracted. Companies seemed to be asking themselves what they were in business for, and deciding that in fact they were not running catering, cleaning and transport firms. Indeed, these are the three areas most frequently to be sub-contracted.

Having read the NEDC/IMS report, one could be forgiven for believing that the nation was embarked on an inextricable march towards widespread sub-contract working. The report notes that, of a survey of 72 firms in the food, engineering, retail and financial sectors, some 70% reported an increase in their sub-contracting arrangements. Overwhelming evidence, one might think.

A fly in the ointment appears in a subsequent report[4] prepared by Anna Pollert of the University of Warwick's Industrial Relations Research Unit. Ms Pollert had, apparently, started out to collect evidence about the operation of the core and periphery model, only to end up somewhat disillusioned as the evidence she received from her survey organisations failed to match that of the NEDC/ IMS study.

Talking of the core and periphery model in the round, Ms Pollert concluded:

"Although superficially persuasive, the model rests on an uncertain basis of confused assumptions and unsatisfactory evidence. The assertion of a new polarisation between core and periphery is misleading. It should be abandoned in favour of a more historically and theoretically informed analysis."

Referring solely to sub-contracting, Ms Pollert is no less agressive. "There is little evidence . . . of a dramatic increase in sub-contracting in the private sector," she concludes, drawing upon an IRRU survey[5] to show that over 60% of respondents had not increased their level of sub-contracting over the previous five years.

The same survey also showed that sub-contracting was nothing new; a staggering 83% of establishment managers already sub-contracted out one service, 39% put out three or more services of which catering and cleaning featured most often.

To add to the confusion, evidence from the food and drink industry showed a *decline* in sub-contracting over the period, whereas in mechanical engineering there was an increase — primarily as a result of an increase in bought-in parts.

At this stage we can draw three conclusions from the survey evidence:

• that sub-contracting is not new;
• that its incidence varies from industry to industry and organisation to organisation; and
• that where it has been recently introduced, this may have been for a variety of reasons — cultural, industrial relations, Government policy — and not just to achieve numerical flexibility or lower costs.

One thing that everyone does seem to be agreed upon is that the jobs that may be sub-contracted have been growing wider. A major study prepared by the Institute of Personnel Management[6] showed that road haulage was the area to be sub-contracted in two-thirds of the organisations using this system of work; followed by cleaning, security and catering.

The IPM concluded:

"We cannot claim that our small sample of case study organisations is representative of what is happening nationally, but the extent to which road haulage has been sub-contracted by these organisations was nevertheless unexpected."

The institute noted the following activities which the organisations in their survey had sub-contracted:

Road transport	Forklift truck maintenance
Catering	Chauffeurs
Cleaning (Office & Industrial)	TV producers
Security	Public relations
Laundry services	Marketing
Maintenance engineering	Market research
Draughtsmen	Personnel
Design engineering	Training
Plumbing	Payroll administration
Carpentry	Gardening
Painting	Word processing
Drain cleaning	Secretarial
Internal mail	Clerical and administrative
Architects	Telephonists
Surveyors	Work study/Industrial
Civil engineering	engineering
Development engineering	Retail management (franchising)
Refrigeration engineering	Data processing staff
Building maintenance	Printing

We now need to assess why employers have sub-contracted elements of their activities.

Why Sub-Contract?

The answer to this question, as far as the NEDC/IMS report was concerned, centred on employers' attempts to maximise numerical flexibility, which is itself a central principle of the core and periphery model.

Anna Pollert, however, was less convinced. Noting a number of other influences affecting an employer's decision to sub-contract, Ms Pollert concluded:

"It may well be that the growth of sub-contracting is most marked where specialist labour is in short supply...and in the public sector, through the privatisation [*sic*] of services. But this form of usage does not illustrate a search for increasing 'numerical flexibility', as is suggested in the 'flexible firm'...A sector specific analysis examining corporate culture, work organisation and product market conditions would provide a more penetrating explanation of these varied and often contrary trends than does the imposition of a labour flexibility argument, or a single managerial imperative."

The point, perhaps, comes down to this, that the decision to move to a core and periphery working system may reflect less the specific policy decision of employers, than their reaction to external conditions over which they have no control. The *reasons* why employers sub-contract some services do not necessarily equate with the *advantages* that accrue to them.

What are the advantages of Sub-Contracting?

Traditionally employers have seen three advantages from sub-contracting. These can be summarised as:

- concentrating resources on core business activities;
- reducing costs whilst increasing flexibility and productivity; and
- enhancing the job security of core employees.

The aim of a decision to concentrate resources on core activities, especially during periods of recession or market volatility, is to transfer some at least of the uncertainties of running a business onto other shoulders. According to the IPM survey, Rank Xerox in Micheldean made the specific policy decision to concentrate on three activities. The result since 1980 has been a reduction in staffing from 4,800 to 1,200, most of the losses occurring in ancillary areas through the elimination or amalgamation of work or through sub-contracting. The company has always used some sub-contractors to even out peaks and troughs in demand, but more recently has sub-contracted external transport, office cleaning, maintenance engineering, civil trades (carpenters, painters, builders) and internal mail.

Even more radical, in a sense, has been the decision of an oil company to sub-contract its secretarial needs to an agency, thus neatly transferring a major headache for London employers. Whilst Cadbury Schweppes found that the speed of technological advances in printing made it more cost effective for them to sub-contract their in-house printing operations.

To these advantages of "sticking to the knitting" can be added the benefits of sub-contracting areas of expertise that the company would otherwise find difficult to manage: the reduction in employment costs and industrial relations problems if someone else is providing the service; the freeing up of capital otherwise invested, for example, in lorry fleets that may be idle for two-thirds of the time; and the more efficient use of expensive expertise if it is only employed as and when needed.

Another major benefit of sub-contracting, to the employer at least, is the savings in costs. It has been estimated that the real cost of employing someone, all things considered, is 50 to 100% above the cost of the base salary. Reducing headcount can therefore make sense. On top of saving a substantial proportion of the add-on costs, because contracts are generally short-term/renewable, employers can control their total labour expenditure via terminating contracts when the service is no longer needed, or by shopping around for a better deal.

Apart from straight cost savings, companies often quote other cost benefits from sub-contracting. These can be expressed as:

- more positive attitudes on the part of sub-contractors and their staff;
- higher productivity;
- greater flexibility to deal with peaks, troughs and reasonable variations;
- few disputes and stoppages;
- less overtime working;
- fewer restrictive practices;
- savings in recruitment and training costs (especially where turnover is high);
- savings in the costs of absence.

Rank Xerox, already referred to, claimed cost savings of around 30% on a budget of £600,000 for external transport operations from their sub-contracting exercise; along with a number of other benefits including substantial savings in add-on employment costs. Similar cost improvements were noted in other sub-contracted departments. The BBC noted that putting out its cleaning and security needs could reduce the costs over in-house provision by up to 30%. Other cost savings arise from reduced overtime payments; indeed, part of Petrofina's decision to use drivers on sub-contracts came from a desire to reduce excessive overtime working.

Some would claim that using sub-contract and other peripheral labour enhances the security of the core employees. Well it might, but the IPM study could only find one example of a company where this was the express aim of the policy. This was Xidex in South Wales in an area of very high unemployment. Otherwise, this altruistic approach to sub-contracting does not apparently figure over much.

The problems of Sub-Contracting

Only the most naïve employer would claim that there are no disadvantages in using sub-contract labour, although it must be said that they seem to feel these are often outweighed by the various benefits outlined above.

The first major problem facing employers concerns the legal status of sub-contractors — a notoriously grey area in tax and employment law terms. Even if the parties to an agreement state that the relationship is a contract for service (as opposed to a contract for services), the courts may decide that the evidence does not support the claim. The difficulties surrounding this entire area probably explain why one rarely sees a labour lawyer on a bicycle. As far as tax is concerned, sub-contractors will only be treated as such provided they did more than 51% of their work for one employer. This clearly has repercussions for employers wishing to buy back a (reduced) level of service from redundant employers, or intending to offer them a guaranteed level of work in their first year of self-employment, as many companies have.

Despite the views of most employers that sub-contractors are more reliable, efficient *etc*, this is by no means the experience of all. One company in the IPM study noted of its sub-contract secretarial staff that

> "this group of employees has been characterised by high absence, high turnover and labour market shortage problems, with the result that a great deal of management time has been spent in recruitment and training."

Clearly, employers must monitor and control sub-contractors in perhaps a slightly more rigorous way than they monitor the performance of their own staff. But here is certainly an example where sub-contracting does not reduce core managerial problems.

A more important problem arising from an overuse of sub-contract labour, both for individual organisations and ultimately the nation at large, relates to training and skill shortages.

The training requirements of some catering and most cleaning staff, the traditional sub-contract labourers, are not great, the work being largely unskilled. Concerns arise, however, when companies choose to sub-contract semi-skilled or even skilled work.

Up to now the training of these latter groups has been the responsibility of employers and Government working together. No-one would argue that hitherto training in the UK has been perfect, far from it, but it was something. The present Government has started the process of putting the responsibility for training firmly in the hands of employers acting voluntarily, despite all the evidence that voluntary action has hardly been successful in the past. If one adds to the scenario a growing band of semi and skilled *self-employed* labour, it is not difficult to foresee a declining trained base of suitable sub-contractors for employers to call on. The irony could well be that larger employers, unwilling to put up with the vagaries of competing for an ever decreasing supply of skilled contractors, will determine to recruit again to ensure their needs are met, thus making the problem even worse for the rest.

This is a problem that has started to occur. The IPM study had this to say:

> "The growth of sub-contracting into non traditional skilled and professional employment fields is too recent a phenomenon to have made much impact on skills training and skills shortage. Nevertheless one organisation, the BBC... was considering steps to overcome potential future problems. The BBC noted that one of the knock-on effects of a greater use of freelancers and contract staff in both technical and production areas would be its implications for the Corporation's traditional training role. Historically, the BBC has done most of the training for the television industry in Britain and, in the light of greater sub-contracting, is now looking at ways of sharing the cost burden with the independent television companies... to ensure that a sufficient volume of training is carried out to meet the needs of the whole industry."

Finally, as personnel managers, we must take account of the effects of sub-contracting on the organisation's employee relations system.

I remember many years ago talking to a down-to-earth industrial relations manager in a manufacturing company about his views on the shorter working week. Expecting him to be opposed to further cuts, I was surprised when he supported a reduced working week on the basis that when the workforce were at home "they weren't causing trouble". Attitudes to sub-contracting and industrial relations sometimes fall into the same category — "It's someone else's problem".

Trade unions are naturally opposed to the use of sub-contract labour which they see as weakening their member base and power. Some have been successful in blocking the use of sub-contractors altogether; others have at least received managerial commitments to consultation on the issue; whilst yet others have agreements that sub-contractors must be members of the same union. Not all unions are opposed, however, especially where sub-contracting underpins a serious attempt on behalf of the parties to reduce excessive overtime.

The biggest problem lies perhaps in the future. Sub-contracting introduced in the teeth of union opposition hardly sets the scene for a calm industrial relations environment. As the IPM and Incomes Data Services concluded in their analysis of contracting out in the NHS and Local Government:[7]

> "In both these major areas of contracting out, Personnel Managers generally look with a certain amount of distaste upon what they were being asked to do. The effects of contracting out have been held to distort and disrupt policies and procedures that have been built up over many years . . . "

They continued

> " . . . and to bear particularly hard on the living conditions of the acknowledged low wage earner section of the workforce."

That, however, is another story.

Conclusion

The major conclusion is probably that sub-contracting has been around for many years; it seems to be growing but not in any concerted or even major way; and the effects of sub-contracting defy any sensible analysis at present because of the lack of comprehensive evidence as to its incidence, social costs, benefits, *etc*, that it has advantages, but that these may eventually be outweighed by the disadvantages.

It is the role of personnel managers to enable organisations to achieve objectives through the best use of their human resource. Sub-contracting is a use of resource which may benefit some organisations, sometimes. At the moment, however, it seems that the biggest bar to the growth of sub-contracting will be imposed by declining training opportunities coupled with high interest rates, which will certainly have a bearing on the viability of many self-employed concerns.

Government please note!

STEVE PALMER
Institute of Personnel Management

References

1 National Economic Development Council, *Changing Working Patterns: how companies achieve flexibility to meet new needs*, NEDO, London: 1986.
2 C Handy, 'The Organisation Revolution and How To Harness It', *Personnel Management*: July 1984, pp 20–23.
3 T J Peters and R H Waterman, *In Search of Excellence*, Harper Row: New York, 1987.
4 A Pollert, *The 'Flexible Firm': A Model in search of reality (or a policy in search of a practice)?*, Warwick Papers in Industrial Relations No 19, University of Warwick: December 1987.
5 P Marginson, et al, *Beyond the Workplace*, Blackwell, Oxford: 1988.
6 C Curson, *Flexible Patterns of Work*, Institute of Personnel Management, London: 1986.
7 *Competitive Tendering in the Public Sector*, Institute of Personnel Management and Incomes Data Services, London: October 1986.

7

Contracting-Out in UK Manufacturing Industry: Recent Developments and Issues

Precis

Over the last decade analyses of the UK labour market have revealed two groups: permanent, full-time employees; and non-permanent, non-full-time employees. In addition to these two groups, the role of service providing and labour-only providing contractors has emerged. Interest in both of these developments starts from a need to understand their nature and extent, and their utility to the fulfilment of full-employment policies.

The purpose of this paper is to demonstrate the changes occurring in "working practices" in UK manufacturing industry with regards to contracting-out, explaining why contracting-out is undertaken and how it is effected. The method adopted has been to undertake a detailed and systematic analysis of the developments occurring on 238 manufacturing sites in the UK over the period October 1981 to October 1988 as recorded in a database developed for the study of organisational change.

The paper concludes that:

1 The extent of contracting-out has increased since October 1981 in terms of the numbers employed, the range of services contracted-out, the number of companies engaged in contracting, and the value of the contracts let.

2 The increase in contracting-out has occurred as a direct result of companies seeking to reduce fixed costs. The rate, scope, selection and usage of contractors are influenced by a range of factors.

3 The increase in the level of contracting-out has been effected by one of two main routes: supplementing or replacing existing on-site resources and services.

4 Nearly 34% of the jobs lost from the manufacturing sites considered were replaced by an increase in employment by contractors.

5 Further study is necessary in order to understand the costs

and benefits of contracting-out to companies, employees and regional economies.

Introduction

Over the past decade increasing interest has been shown in understanding not only the shape and nature of work itself, but also different terms, conditions and status of participants in the UK labour market. Since the late 1970s an increasing proportion of the UK labour market has been made up of non-permanent, non-full-time employees (commonly known as "flexible workers") which now account for 34% of the total. In four industrial sectors the proportion of "flexible workers" is nearly, or more than, 50% of the total: *eg*, agriculture — 60%; construction — 42%; distribution, hotels and catering — 52%; and other services — 42%. In contrast to these relatively high levels, manufacturing industry would appear to make a relatively small use of "flexible workers": *eg*, chemicals and minerals — 9%; metal goods, engineering and vehicles — 10%; and other manufacturing — 19%.[1] All of these figures relate to a "flexible workforce" which contains temporary employees, part-time employees, and the self-employed. It does not specifically consider those organisations which employ people on a full-time basis but sell their time on either a temporary or part-time basis to a third party. Nor do these figures consider those companies whose service directly requires the provision of labour on the host company's site. It is the purpose of this paper to consider this part of the labour market which is made up of full-time employees which are provided on a flexible basis.

The provision of full-time employees by contractors — predominantly for support services, such as cleaning, washrooms, waste, linen, workwear, communications, distribution, plant-hire, maintenance, security, manned guarding *etc* — has seen the growth of multiple support service companies: for example BET, now owns 500 such companies employing 120,000 people.[2] On the specialist contractor side, companies such as the Compass Group have developed to supply the employee and institutional catering markets which are now worth £3.5 billion in the UK. these two catering markets are dominated by two companies and are followed by a further 38 companies with 20 or more outlets.[3] One market which is amongst that catered for by support service contractors is on-site maintenance which is highly skilled work and critical to the success of manufacturing: *eg*, on one of ICI Chemical and Polymers middle-sized sites, maintenance failures cost them £6.7m or 29%

of their total cost of non-conformity.[4] Contract maintenance has therefore had a direct impact upon the profitability of a site far in excess of most other services supplied by a contractor.

Both the overall increase in the numbers of "flexible workers" and that of contractors have been developments directly related to the drive of manufacturing companies, amongst others, to reduce the level of fixed costs and to shift as many costs as possible on to a variable basis. This drive reduces the level of burden upon a business before it can recover its overhead and declare a profit. During the first 3–4 years of the 1980s it was evident that manufacturing companies reduced direct and especially indirect costs in line with those which could be carried by their level of capacity utilisation. This period also saw a major effort to reduce the cost of in-house support services usually through their replacement by contractors which specialised in a particular support service or range of support services. Invaribly the reduction in cost was achieved through paying low rates of pay.[5]

In the second half of the 1980s, manufacturing companies have sought to raise their internal levels of efficiency by reorganising individual jobs and by changing the orientation of the sites along product/market lines. This change to focus a manufacturing site along customer/business lines has directly lead to an increase in the number of job holders with the authority to let contracts for support services which might have previously been supplied by a site central services function. Thus the growth in the use of contractors has been fuelled by the rapid adjustment of manufacturers to match fixed costs with levels of capacity utilisation and the reorganisation of sites along business lines. In addition to these factors there has been the uptake of new technologies which have demanded "new" skills and knowledge which are in short supply, the buying of plant and equipment on lease, *etc.*[6] These factors are considered in Section 5.

Amongst the many aspects of contractors and changes in the UK labour market, the specific purpose of this paper is to demonstrate the changes occurring in working practices (especially in relation to the growth of self-employment and the formation of the "flexible economy") in UK manufacturing industry with regard to "contracting-out", explaining why contracting-out is undertaken and how it is effected. In meeting this overall purpose the paper seeks to address the following issues:

- to demonstrate the extent and nature of contracting-out in the UK manufacturing industry since October 1981;

- to explain why the extent and nature of contracting-out in UK manufacturing industry has changed since October 1981;
- to illustrate how the extent and nature of contracting-out in UK manufacturing industry has been effected at site level since October 1981.

Each of these issues are addressed in separate sections, while the immediately subsequent section to this one considers the data upon which the paper is based.

Database

Since October 1981, initially at the Technical Change Centre (1981–1986) and now at the City University Business School, the development and diffusion of changes in working practices and associated changes in pay, hours of work, use of contractors, *etc*, on 238 manufacturing sites employing 237,380 people have been continuously monitored by the author. The sites are operated by 128 companies which in total employed 1,665,060 in 1987/88 (in 1979/80 they employed 2,314,310 people, a decline of 23%). During the period October 1981 to March 1988, the 128 companies have closed 108 sites, opened a further 23, and continued to manufacture on another 401 sites (additional to the 238 covered in the research database). Table 7.1 details the industrial sectors of both the companies and sites in the Research database.

Thirty of the 128 companies are constituents of the FT100 Share Index, while 47 are amongst the top 100 exporters from the UK (1986/87 amounting to £27,300 million, up by 77% since 1980/81). Of the 238 sites considered, 37 have declared no redundancies, while 53 have reduced the numbers employed by 50% or more since 1980/81.

In terms of bargaining arrangements, 20 conduct pay and all other negotiations at company level, while the other 108 conduct all bargaining at site level. In the case of 24 of the sites' bargaining arrangements, the company operates only at one plant, and in seven cases the companies do not recognise trade unions for bargaining purposes. Only three of the companies have single union agreements with a further 29 having a "federation" of process, craft and staff unions who bargain together with their respective employers. The relevant information has been collected through interviews (2600 in all), observations, questionnaires, and examination of company documentation. On 54 of the 238, detailed, long-term examinations have been conducted in the following industrial sectors: food, drinks and tobacco (on 12 sites); chemical and allied products (12 sites); plastics and rubber (2 sites); coal and petroleum products (4 sites); glass, cement and bricks (6 sites); paper (10 sites); and other (1 site). In four cases the complete engineering craft and process operator negotiations have been attended.

TABLE 7.1
Industrial Sector Coverage of Research Database

Industrial Sector		Companies		Sites	
SIC		No.	%	No.	%
3	Food, drinks & tobacco	29	23	71	30
5	Chemical & allied products	28	22	52	22
19	Plastic & rubber	14	11	23	9.5
7,8,9,11	Engineering	22	17	29	12
6	Metal manufacture	4	3	5	2
4	Coal & petroleum products	6	5	9	4
16	Glass, cement & bricks	12	9	23	9.5
18	Paper	6	8	19	8
–	Other	5	4	7	3
	TOTAL	128	–	238	–

As a result of the research activity (Table 7.1), data have been collected on the use of contractors on the 238 sites covered in the research database. The nature of these data are as follows: number of contractors used, number of contracts let, value of the contracts let, length of the contract let, vetting criteria used when assessing a contractor, numbers of employees used by the contractors on the host 238 sites, date of entry on to the host site, *etc*.

In terms of coverage of manufacturing activity, the 238 sites covered in the database represent 4.1% of all full-time employers, or 4.8% of all full-time employers equivalents. The 128 companies operating these 238 sites employ 33.7% of all permanent full-time employees in UK manufacturing (Table 7.2).

TABLE 7.2
Employment Coverage of Research Database

Industrial Sector	Total No. of Employees	Database No. of Employees	% Coverage
2 Other mineral & ore extraction etc.	769700	77660	10.1
3 Metal goods, engineering & vehicles etc.	2198000	57600	2.6
4 Other manufacturing industries	2057100	102120	4.9
TOTAL	5024800	237380	4.7

The extent and nature of Contracting-out in UK Manufacturing Industry

The purpose of this section is:

- to identify the range of contractors providing support services to the 238 sites in the research database since October 1981;
- to establish the *extent* of contracting-out on the 238 sites in the research database since October 1981.

Before considering the range of contractors providing support services to the manufacturing sites, it is important to clarify the type of contractors covered in this research report. The contractors covered are those which provide their service on a host site through the provision of labour and supporting resources. Excluded are those contractors which provide their services off-site — *eg* machine shops, motor rewinds, pump overhauls, *etc* — while these same contractors might also provide a direct labour contracting service to the site. In cases such as this, those employees undertaking off-site work are not included in the employment figures used below.

In all, 117 different types of contractors have been identified, which can be categorised in a number of ways. First, the general contracting services provided can be used (see Table 7.3) which identifies six main categories. It is also possible to categorise the contractors by the exact nature of the service provided in terms of the following factors:

- continuous provision of a service for all of the site;
- specialist service;
- labour broker only;
- balance of service provided on-site to off-site provision;
- capital base of the contractor;
- contracting is the core service provided by company, or is, for example, a development from an existing manufacturing base;
- nature of contract held: *eg*, fixed term/lump sum, day-work, *etc*;
- skills and knowledge base of employees of contractors' employees;
- on-site equivalent exists

TABLE 7.3
Number of Different Contractors Identified

General Contracting Services Provided	Number of Types of Contractor Identified
1 Site services	33
2 Finance	4
3 Personnel	14
4 Production	9
5 Warehousing & Distribution	5
6 Engineering & Maintenance	52
TOTAL	117

It is evident from the range of contractors identified that almost all manufacturing services can be contracted out, and the exact mix depends upon the nature of the manufacturing site examined. By far the most frequently identified contracting service provided, irrespective of the manufacturing process involved, was catering. In catering the economics of scale in the purchasing of food stuffs coupled with low wages (relative to the average paid in manufacturing industry) has given contract caterers a large cost advantage when compared to their in-house equivalent. Companies such as Gardner Merchant, a part of the Trusthouse Forte Group, now employs over 34,000 staff and operates with the majority of major UK companies (84 of the top 100), and currently sells and operates within over 4000 companies in all.

Contrast the almost ubiquitous contract catering provision to that of the high skill, high technology services provided by such companies as Roxby Engineering. Companies like Roxby provide specialist services which directly impact upon manufacturing performance and include the following:

- plant operation and maintenance;
- training;
- process and instrument commissioning;
- technical resources;
- corrosion control engineering;
- materials management;
- instrument and electrical installation;
- inspection services.

The Extent of Contractor Usage

Measuring the *extent* of the use of contractors and how the level of usage has changed is not straightforward, and there are a number of options available:

- number of contractor companies used;
- number of contracts let;
- total value of the contracts let;
- number of people employed by contractors (absolute numbers and relative to those employed by the host site).

None of these four measures is ideal. For example, of the 238 sites in the research database, 183 have made greater use of contractors since 1981. The measure used here is the number of services provided by contractors. Of these 183 sites, 76 (42%) have increased the use of contractors as a direct result of a company policy to reduce forcibly the total numbers employed by a fixed, across-the-board proportion. For example, in the case of one company a "10%/10 %" policy has been adopted, *ie* 10% of all labour requirements will be provided by contractors, and a further 10% will be provided by their own staff through working overtime. By adopting this policy it is possible to reduce rapidly operating costs to allow profits growth to be maintained and also to maintain share value on the New York Stock Exchange.

If the contractors are sorted by both the value and the rate of increase in usage (assuming that costs have increased equally across contracting services) the following hierarchy emerges:

1st   Engineering and maintenance

2nd Transport, distribution and warehousing
3rd Site services

In terms of the numbers of people employed (both actual numbers of individuals employed and in terms of full-time equivalents) the following overall picture emerges:

TABLE 7.4
**Changes in the Level of Employment in
Manufacturing Industry and Contractors, 1981–1988**

	MANUFACTURING		CONTRACTORS	
	Absolute Numbers	*Full-time Equivalents*	*Absolute Numbers*	*Full-time Equivalents*
1981	395633	431240*		37499△
1988	202025	237380**		59345△

Notes:
  * *Includes an average of 9% overtime*
** *Includes an average of 17.5% overtime*
△ *It has not proved possible to separate out absolute numbers or individuals employed, nor the levels of overtime worked by those employees, and therefore this figure represents the full-time equivalents employed.*

In addition to the 59345 contractor personnel employed on an average base on the 238 sites in the research database, there were a further 4510 people employed on average at their head offices or equivalent. These 4510 people had been allocated on a pro rata basis to those employed in the field and does not represent the total non-field based employment of the contractors.

In considering the absolute and full-time numbers of contractors employed in the 238 sites it is important to realise that these are annual average figures. The actual level numbers of contractor personnel can fluctuate by 50% or more over a year. Table 5 details the levels of maintenance contractor personnel on site during 1988 and the forecast levels for 1989 and 1990.
  The majority of the contractor services are provided by a little over 800 companies whose business on the 238 sites (*cont'd page* 63)

TABLE 7.5
Quarterly Variations in Maintenance Contractor Usage

Time			Contractor Manpower Levels
1988	1st	Qtr	1000
	2nd		1300
	3rd		1800
	4th		2000 (ann. av. 1525)
1989	1st	Qtr	2200
	2nd		2450
	3rd		2250
	4th		1900 (ann. av. 2200)
1990	1st	Qtr	1850
	2nd		900
	3rd		950
	4th		1250 (ann. av. 1238)

Source: Oil and Chemical complex in the UK

TABLE 7.6
Source of Main Contractor Companies

"Origin"	No. of Contractor Company
Established on site previously	421
Companies new to site, but in existence pre-1981	398
New Companies post-1981	72
New Companies post-1981 set-up by ex-employees of host site	38
New Companies post-1981 (takeover, 6 set up by ex-employees; 35 were new companies)	41

Notes:
The new companies fall into three main types: major management buyouts creating national companies; management buyouts which create single customer contractors; and, other companies often not set-up as contracting companies initially. By far the majority of management buyouts fall into the minor management buyouts of the site garage or canteen and then contracting it back to the site.

was worth £1.235 billion in 1988. The remaining £309 million worth of contractor services were provided by over 6000 other companies, most of which have only contracts with one of the 238 sites. The 819 contract companies which supply the bulk of the contract services identified had the following "origins":

If the research database is divided into nine industrial sectors and one other catch-all category, the large difference in the use of contractors is identified. Three levels of contractor usage (in terms of employment) can be seen to emerge (see Table 7.7):

"high"   in   chemical and allied products
                    metal manufacturer
                    coal and petroleum products

"medium"   in   paper
                    engineering
                    glass, cement and bricks

"low"   in   plastics and rubber
                    food, drinks and tobacco
                    other

TABLE 7.7
Variations in Contractor Employment Levels
by Industrial Sector

Industrial Sector	*Contractor Levels**		*Own Numbers Employed**	
	1981 %	1987 %	1981 %	1987 %
Food, drink & tobacco	3	10	97	90
Chemicals & allied products	18	40	82	60
Plastic & rubber	10	11	90	89
Engineering	7	17	93	83
Metal Manufacture	10	31	90	69
Coal & petroleum products	17	29	83	71
Glass, cement & bricks	13	15	87	85
Paper	14	18	86	82
Other	9	11	91	89
Average	12	20	88	80

These figures are full-time equivalents and are averaged over the two years of 1981 and 1987.

It was noted earlier that there are a number of ways in which to measure the extent of contractor usage, and the absolute size of contractors. Similarly it is equally difficult to assess the size and significance of the shift in terms of the balance of contractor to host-site employment. A number of the factors which are relevant here are:[9]

Productivity growth: On the 238 host sites continued efforts have been made to raise productivity through the introduction of new shift patterns, new structures to the working day, new information systems for engineering and production, use of total quality programmes, the move to CIB/CIM/SCADA, *etc*. Each of these changes represent an investment in organisational and system technology which have removed the need for some work and reduced the frequency and duration of other tasks. Adding to this has been the move to increase the overlap of related roles both across and up the organisation.[10] Together these moves have reduced the need for about 50–60,000 jobs, whilst output is significantly higher than in 1981 and a greater proportion produced to the specified quality. These drives to raise productivity have in the main been focussed upon manufacturing and not the support services. The productivity of support services has been raised by reducing its cost by contracting it out at least in part. Thus the improved productivity (of about 20–40% over the 1981–87 period) on the sites studied tends to overstate the shift to contractors[11] in terms of employment, which is further compounded by the fact that many of the services contracted out are relatively labour intensive, *eg* cleaning, catering, *etc*.

Capital investment: Leaving aside the usual "revenue capital" expenditure, £5595m has been invested on the 238 sites. This investment has required much reduced numbers of people to operate the plants, and not greatly increased the capacity of the sites. A number of issues emerge from justification of the capital (short payback period and reduced capacity utilisation to break even) and the resourcing of the operation of the capital once commissioned. In the later case there has been a growth in the use of equipment manufacturers, equipment suppliers and specialist contractors supplying skills and knowledge to maintain process control systems and devices. In part this form of contract has occurred at a time of the rapid uptake of process control systems, which has also been a tendency on wholly new sites (of which there are 18 in the research database), to contract out the bulk of the support services and to keep the host site full-time employee numbers to a minimum. Again, these actions tend to depress the number of full-time equivalent jobs on the host sites in relation to contractor employee numbers.

Shift working: At present about 12% of all employees in manufacturing industry work shifts. Only 3 of the 238 sites do not work shifts, and of the 235 that do, most work discontinuous shift operations (145 in all). These shift patterns vary in length and in structure. By far the bulk of the contractors (92%) do not work shifts. Thus the day workforce of the host sites can feel they are being dominated by contractors when they might only represent 30–35% of the total day workforce. This time dependent element in the balance of host site and contractor employees numbers is not reflected in the Table 7.7.

Length of the Working Day and the Working Week: Attempting to move between total hours worked and the number of full-time equivalents is complicated by the length of the working day (on average in the sample for host site employees it is 7¾ hours on a 39 hours week). The shortest week worked is 35 hours. This means that overtime is worked earlier in the host companies than in the contractors by at least one hour difference. The figures are still further complicated by the differences in attended hours, worked hours, and paid hours. Often there are discrepancies of 2–2½ hours between these various categories which again affects the move between gross hours and the numbers employed either on the host sites and in particular the numbers of people employed by contractors. The tendency here would be to inflate the actual number of individuals employed by contractors.

Level of Shutdown Work: Many of the sites in the sample engage in annual and less frequent shutdown of individual plants and/or complexes of plants. As is evident from the figures in Table 7.5, the numbers of contractor employees on a site vary throughout a year and from a year. If, for example, all of the sites in the survey were to engage in a major shutdown in the same year (and using the figures from their most recent shutdown) the number of contractor employees in 1988 would be 87,462 (an increase of 28,117 or 47%). Here there is also an increase in the hours worked by the host site employees, but no longer as high as it had been in the 1970s. Most of the shutdown overtime hours have either "exported" to contractors who now undertake the work or to the introduction of temporary shifts. Hence the figures for 1981 would include some element of overtime working on shutdown which is now undertaken by contractors. In the oil refining industry alone this might account for as many as 175 full-time equivalents per site.

Overtime: The calculation and amount of overtime distorts both the host site and contractor employee numbers. For example, the host site employee numbers are inflated by 35,355 if the standard work-week (taken as 39 hours) is divided by the gross number of hours paid. A distinction also needs to be made between worked and paid hours of overtime. In the calculations undertaken to construct Table 7.4 paid overtime figures have been used rather than worked. The difference between the two can be significant where the pre-determined number of paid hours can far exceed the number of worked hours. This complication in the figures tends to inflate the number of full-time equivalent employees on the host company sites.

Non-establishment Employees: The employee figures used in Table 7.4 are based on the annual average of the numbers employed and not the establishment or budget numbers. Also excluded are supernumeraries such as YTS trainees, apprentices, graduate trainees, *etc*. The vast majority of these supernumeraries are employed on the host company sites (about 4% of the total).

Non-counted Contractors: All of the contractors' employee numbers in Table 7.4 are employed on the host company sites to provide a service. Thus, excluded from the numbers are those contractors who do not deliver their service via their employees on the host company site. For example, if an employment agency were to provide a team of people to assist in a special product launch on-site then they would be included in the study. However, they would be excluded if the materials were moved off-site and handled by a third party contract packer. It has not been possible to pursue all of the latter types of arrangements to establish the full extent of contractor employee numbers.

Other Hidden Factors: The figures in Table 7.4 do not in any way reveal the extent of contractor turnover, the seasonality component of the total contractor base, the balance between permanent and temporary employees amongst the total numbers of full-time equivalents, and at lower level, the turnover of contractor employee and the quality of the jobs they perform. Again for the purpose of this paper, it has not been possible to establish in detail the exact nature of these "hidden" factors.

Despite the difficulties and complexities of disentangling the exact numbers of contractor employees, it is evident that the extent and range of contractors have risen since 1981. It is also evident that a significant proportion of the work undertaken by the contractors represents a direct substitution of services previously provided by the host site's employees. The range and size of the contractor base on site is strongly dependent upon the industry sector of the site. A significant proportion of the larger contractor companies operating on the 238 sites were "new" companies established after 1981 (151, or 16%). The next section considers the factors which explain the use and variations in use of contractors on manufacturing sites.

Factors influencing the use of Contractors

There are three main groups of factors which influence the use of contractors:

(1) those factors which influence the *rate* at which a manufacturing company makes use of contractors: *eg*, the rate at which an in-house service is replaced by a contractor;
(2) those factors which influence, and to some extent determine the *scope* of the work which a contractor can undertake;
(3) those factors which influence the general and specific *selection* and *usage* of contractors.

The purpose of this section is to examine each of these three groups of factors in turn.

Rate

By far the biggest single factor giving rise to the greater use of contractors is costs. Between 1979 and 1984 the vast majority of manufacturing companies sought to bring manufacturing costs (in particular by reducing fixed costs and increasing variable costs) in line with capacity utilisation. One of the routes taken to achieve this reduction in costs, and a change in its structure, was to greatly reduce the number of employees on site and supplement any peaks in demand with contract staff. This shift between own and contract staff was further speeded-up by the perception that contract staff are more productive than own staff, and was demonstrably cheaper in many cases. The exact size of the difference in productivity between these two main groups of employees was between 7–8 and 15–20% as measured by "tool-in-hand-time". What this rather crude productivity revealed in the oil refining industry was that contract staff were controlled, resourced and managed much more closely: *eg*, jobs were planned, permits were available, *etc*.[12]

The relative cheapness of contractors primarily arises from the bidding-up of wages for people in support jobs not directly related to manufacturing: *eg*, security, catering, secretarial services, *etc*. The comparable rates of pay for these support jobs might be 50% lower in some cases, especially in the high paying industrial sectors: *eg*, oil refining and chemicals. Allied to this direct cost comparison on wages, contracting companies have been bidding for contracts with a fixed price, *ie* the company letting the contract has established what it can afford against a "given" cost base. The growth of fixed price contracts which (almost) guarantees a service at given cost is very attractive to production and site managers who are assessed on conformance to budget and cost reduction.[13]

Just as immediate cost reduction was the spur to many manufacturing companies to increase the usage of contractors, the same approach to productivity improvement has had within it its own barriers. The most readily apparent features of these "barriers" are the lack of resources to allow further organisational size and structure changes to be made. For example, on one chemical site, manufacturing costs were rapidly reduced over the period 1980–1984 primarily by reducing the numbers employed (by about 460, or 38%). Over the following two years volumes increased, but the numbers employed were held static and reduced where possible. By 1987 and 1988 the now "buoyant" demand for the sites output could only be achieved by working high levels of overtime (in excess of 25 %) and by employing contract staff on a full-time basis to supplement their own full-time staff. The high overtime levels have now become a "cost" which the company wishes to reduce and is also an industrial relations barrier and problem. First, the barrier comes from the now inflated rates of pay which after two years have become the accepted, normal rate of pay. This has inflated the price of change during their most recent negotiations which are proposing to increase the base rate of pay for the majority, based upon the acquisition and use of additional skills. It is already possible for all staff on site to improve their personal rate of pay almost as and when they like. Second, the problems that arise from the possible reduction in earnings through the increased use of contractors. Together these two factors have (almost) forced the company into a corner as regards to making their next changes to improve long-term site costs. This position had been arrived at through the concentration upon reducing costs irrespective of the long-term implications and the use of contractors as a part of this policy. The net of this policy has lead to a dependence upon a contracting company who are using their position to increase the value of their contract which was initially a day-work based one. One conclusion to draw from this brief example is that the over rapid move to contractors without a long-term view is not without its complications, and can present a series of barriers to making future changes.

Two particular routes are discernible through which the rapid introduction of contractors has been affected. First, there is the wholesale withdrawal from some support services and their replacement by contractors: *eg*, catering, security, transport, *etc*. In those cases where significant assets are involved — *eg*, a warehouse, a transport fleet, *etc* — the transition to a contractor supplier base might occur through a management buyout or a sell-off to a contractor company. Second, there is the large scale reduction of the host site employee numbers and the retreat from particular types of "peak loads" of work, like shutdown work, capital work, *etc*. In this case contractors are progressively introduced on to a site as and when appropriate work arises which can be parcelled-up and contracted out as a lump sum/fixed price contract.

Scope

While there may be immediate economic pressures to consider the greater use of contractors to reduce operating costs at least in the short term, the actual scope of the work or service a contractor can undertake or provide is determined by the nature of the production process and the exact characteristics of the work to be undertaken. These comments might appear to contradict the very large range of contractor types identified in Section 4 (see Table 7.3). Earlier in this paper it was established that it is possible to contract out all services to manufacturing and even the manufacture and producing of the product itself. However it is extremely rare for all manufacturing services to be contracted out, and there is seen to be a need for a "mixed economy" approach to the resourcing of manufacturing and associated services by balancing in-house with contract personnel. It is these factors which influence the balance between in-house and contract personnel in terms of the scope of work/service undertaken/provided which forms the basis of the following paragraphs.

The scope for the use of contractors in any organisation can be divided into two main types:

(1) those which directly support the core product or service of the host organisation;
(2) those which provide a general support service common to most host organisations.

The factors which influence the use of contractors in category (1) are quite different from those in category (2). For example, the nature of the production process does not influence the decision to contract out catering other than the size and deployment of the catering services, for example coping with shift workers and shutdown working; whereas a production process which operates on a continuous basis (24 hours per day, 365 days a year) means that annual and less frequent shutdowns will probably be necessary, but might not be wholly open to contractors because of the specialist nature of the work involved. In addition there may be security reasons (commercial confidentiality) which also limit the possible involvement of contractors. Another significant feature of the production process which also influences the use of contractors is the physical size and integration of the plant. The overhaul of a plastic injection moulding machine which is a small free-standing machine, can be undertaken by one or two people and so can be handled either in-house or by contractors. Whereas the full overhaul of a catalytic cracking complex occurs every three to four years and involves upwards of 800 contract personnel supplemented by in-house staff.

Related to the physical size of the plant and the size and frequency of the shutdown is the criticality and cost of interrupting the production process. The cost of lost production from a glass plant, chemicals plant, oil refining, and paper mill are extremely high (in many £000 per hour) and so the relative cost of heavily resourcing a shutdown is small. For example, a 10 million ton per annum capacity oil refinery, operating with a crude oil feedstock costing $15–16 per barrel, loses $50–60,000 per hour in profit for its owners. Hence a 28 day or 42 day shutdown would lose between $33.6–40.3m and $50.4–60.5m in profit. Thus the cost of the shutdown which might range between $10–12m (up to $80–100m if major modifications are being undertaken) is seen as being small, and if an extra $2 or 3m. can win back a few days on the shutdown schedule, it is often seen as a worthwhile investment. What is critical in such a situation is the keeping of the shutdown period to a minimum and running the shutdown within a known period. Remember having a major production unit out for a period requires the building-up of stocks and in some cases buying-in supplies from other sites or even other companies. Products stock-piling is an expensive exercise particularly if the value of the product is falling due to changes in the price of crude oil. In both 1986 and 1987 two oil refineries wrote-off their "profits" (failed to satisfy their manufacturing margins) for the year as a direct result of poor shutdown performance.

In order to understand the use of contractors and the type of work they can, and do perform, it is necessary to know the commercial contract of that work. The factors influencing the perceived cost and value of a catering or security contract company are distinctly different from those of an engineering contractor. In large part this is due to the very direct impact an engineering contractor can have upon the performance of a production process and the fortunes of a manufacturing site. It is also much easier to directly relate the contribution (added value) of the engineering contractor's service to the overall business performance of a manufacturing site.

Based upon the discussion presented above it is possible to determine a typology relating contractor work scope and role to the production process and product type. The typology of contractors operating contexts offered in Figure 7.1 provides more than just a means of describing the current distribution of contracting activity, but it also indicates where labour intensive, relatively low and high paid contracting work occurs. The other point to note is that some manufacturing processes are typified by large fluctuations in their requirements for labour, have a continuous production cycle, and are capital and resource intensive, have high cost penalties for starting-up and closing-down the process, and all make use of sophisticated control systems. Examples of the industries with these characteristics are:

- generation of electricity and gas;
- the separation of hydrocarbons and chemicals by fractional distillation;
- the extraction, refraction and forming of metals;

FIGURE 7.1
Categorisation of Product Types, Production Processes and Contractor Usage

PRODUCTION PROCESS	JOB ◄———— BATCH———— ASSEMBLY———► CONTINUOUS ORDER PROCESS
PRODUCT TYPE	DISCRETE-PART PRODUCT, MANY MATERIAL INPUTS SINGLE OR FEW MATERIALS SERVICES—JOINT PRODUCTS
CONTRACTOR USAGE	EQUAL POTENTIAL FOR USING SERVICE SUPPORT ◄————————————————————————► CONTRACTORS INCREASING SIZE OF POTENTIAL ROLE FOR ————————————————————————► ENGINEERING CONTRACTORS ON MAINTENANCE/ SHUTDOWN WORK

- the production of glass, paper, plastics, paint, rubber, and cement;
- the manufacturing and processing of food and drinks.

Other industries are increasingly acquiring these characteristics — *eg*, car and household goods manufacturers — but are unlikely to adopt the contractor user practices of existing process manufacturing companies (see Table 7.7).

Selection and Usage

The range of factors relevant here can be divided into two main groups:

(1) those factors relevant to the actual selection of a specific contractor and their subsequent retention;
(2) those factors relevant to the physical use of contractors, for example availability, industrial relations impact, *etc.*

There are ten common criteria which are used in the selection of individual contractors. They are:

1 Financial — commercial viability, failures, "company house" checks, limits;
2 Insurance — cover, guarantees;
3 Organisation — evolution, links;
4 Extent Sub-Contractors Used — prices and work quality;
5 Personnel Policies — health and safety, industrial relations, rates of pay, recruitment, training;
6 Facilities — QC/QA policies, resources at base, *etc*;
7 Track Record — at other company sites, other clients;
8 Systems — work estimating, records, *etc.*
9 "Modus Operandi" — Social; and,
10 Formal Authorisation of Firms — supplier code controls (*cont'd page* 74).

TABLE 7.8
Steps in the Control of Contractors

(1)	Identification of needs	(17)	Site control
(2)	Market research	(18)	Progress — programme
(3)	Past experience	(19)	Critical dates
(4)	Initial experience	(20)	Co-ordination
(5)	Short list	(21)	Partial completion
(6)	Statistical appraisal	(22)	Commissioning
(7)	Pre-tender interviews	(23)	Snagging
(8)	Tender lists	(24)	Completion
(9)	Tender period	(25)	Hand over – acceptance
(10)	Tender appraisal	(26)	Documentation
(11)	Post-tender meeting	(27)	Maintenance period
(12)	Contract clarification	(28)	Remedial works
(13)	Contract	(29)	Final acceptance
(14)	Programme	(30)	Release or retention
(15)	Critical dates	(31)	Liability period
(16)	Start on site	(32)	Disputes

(*Steps 22, 23, 25, 27, 28 and 31 all relate to those steps incurred when installing new plant and equipment. Equivalent or similar steps exist in other contractor control processes.*)

It is these ten criteria which form part of the contractor control procedures which many companies use and which can be divided up into 32 steps (32 discrete steps were identified in the course of the work undertaken for the preparation of this report). While it is not the objective of this report to examine the day-to-day issues of engaging and managing contractors, it is useful to realise that the successful move to increase the use of contractors can only occur relatively slowly, especially when the "needs" of a site are only imperfectly known and understood (see Table 7.8).

The selection, on-going management and monitoring of contractors is a continuous process attempting to raise the level of performance of contractors. Where many companies fail to manage the relationship with contractors is in not having an adequate (if any) audit or performance monitoring procedures. Hence, the periodic review of contractors for contract extensions is not a very effective process.

In addition to the specific factors which influence the selection of an individual contractor, there are a series of other factors which also influence the selection and use of contractors. The most significant of these factors are:

> *Nature of Site*: The location of the site directly affects the availability of contractors in the local area and the competition for the available contractors. For example, the availability and demand for engineering contractors in the South East is significantly higher than in, say, the North West; while the demand for such contractors is a direct function of the structure of the local industrial base and the level of demand for the output of the companies that make up that industrial base. First, there are direct effects of high demand for contractors which affect contractor usage rates which changes one of the major benefits of using contractors: low wage rates. Second, a high buoyancy in the local economy often means that "contractors" can find alternative sources of work. For example, maintenance contractors could undertake engineering construction work: in the case of engineering manufacturing companies, and especially those involved in steel fabrication of vessels, reactors, columns and boilers which will fill in for the lack of work with maintenance engineering work. Thus the notion of primary and secondary contractors is quite an important one to explain why the population of contracting companies varies through time.
>
> The physical remoteness of a site also affects the availability, and willingness of contractors to take on some

projects. Resourcing the development at Sellafield or Fawley are quite different than doing similar projects in North West London or Wigan. On the reverse side, the availability of high quality and reliable contractors does in fact lead to the greater use of contractors. For example, comparing the use of contractors by five identical food processing factories it is evident that the use of contractors is largely determined by the availability of skilled labour. Comparing the factories in Glasgow and North West London reveals that London factories make much greater use of contractors for high and low skilled work because of the difficulty of recruiting and retaining staff, while the Glasgow factory tends to make greater use of specific, high skilled mechanical engineering contractors. Most of the electrical and electronic skills are supplied in-house at the Glasgow factory. The use of contractors (especially as regards engineering and maintenance work) is strongly influenced by the buoyancy and make-up of the local labour market which shapes the price, supply and demand for labour.

Nature of the Company: A most noticeable contrast between sites and companies in their use of contractors lies in their age, origin and ownership. It is particularly noticeable that UK owned companies operating on sites in excess of 50 years old have developed a large internal infra-structure to support their manufacturing operations, *eg*, printing of cartons and labels, central engineering workshops, transport fleets, *etc*. Often these support resources were developed at a time when there was little external supply, and the accepted wisdom of the day was to develop both vertically and integrated businesses. Companies such as Unilever are examples of this approach. Their US counterparts, like Procter and Gamble, bought their way into the UK detergents, edible fats and oils, and soaps businesses and never developed the same support infra-structure. P and G concentrated its efforts upon the manufacturing and marketing of its products.

As a result of these differences in the "nature of the company" the starting points in making use of contractors varies greatly, and the increased use of contractors is not uniform.

Nature of the Market Served: The past decade has witnessed very large changes in the logistics of manufacturing covering sourcing/purchasing, materials management and physical distribution. Taking these areas together they represent an average 21% of value added for European firms (8.6% for transportation; 4.4% for warehousing; 4.8% for inventory carrying costs; and 3.2% for administration) and it has been the objective of all the companies in the research database to reduce these costs.[14] Contractors have played a major role in helping to reduce these costs as they have specialised in finding ways to make best use of break-bulk centres, utilization of loads, and high bay and automated warehouses. In addition to these changes many of the major retailers have also directly affected warehousing and transportation for fast-moving consumer goods through the introduction of large centrally-located facilities to serve their stores (often out-of-town, and increasing in size). For some industries, *eg*, food, drinks, tobacco, soap, detergents, non-ethical pharmaceuticals, *etc*. it has meant an almost retreat from on-site warehousing and in-company transport fleets.

The move to the use of physical distribution contractors has taken on two main forms: (i) the removal of on-site warehousing and the selling-off of the transport fleet and the provision of both services through a third party; and (ii), the provision of labour and management by a third party to run the on-site warehouse: *eg* in feminine hygiene products, soft and hard tissues (toilet rolls, kitchen towels), manufacturers have gone down this route.

Not all manufacturing processes and products are amenable to contractors handling their physical distribution (for example, pipeline distribution of gases, oils, petrol, or cable distribution of power or information), but the majority of companies in the research database now make use of some third party. With the growth of some physical distribution companies — *eg* TNT and DHL — they can now compete with the Post Office on many routes.

Nature of Manufacturing Cost Structure: A recurrent theme throughout this paper has been the increased use of contractors to reduce fixed costs. Those manufacturing companies where the fixed costs are high relative to total costs, have in particular sought ways to transfer fixed costs to variable costs, and to reduce the absolute size of the costs as well. Taking two contrasting industries, chemicals and frozen foods, the importance of the manufacturing cost structure in influencing contractors can be illustrated. In Table 7.9, the manufacturing cost structure of a chemical site is detailed where it is evident that one of the largest fixed controllable costs is maintenances. Hence, a large effort has been put into identifying ways of reducing maintenance costs through the use of contractors. The other major costs of energy and manufacturing are not so readily amenable to reduction through increased contractor usage.

TABLE 7.9
Financial Structure of a Chemical Manufacturing Site

Sales £221.5 Mn			*Costs* £71.5 Mn		*Maintenance* £12 Mn	
Costs (value added) £71.5 Mn	32%	Manufacturing & Admin. £34 Mn	47%	Overheads £2.16 Mn	18%
				Labour £2.76Mn	23%
Raw Material & Fuel £101 Mn	46%	Maintenance £12 Mn	17%		
				Materials £2.88 Mn	24%
Operating Profit £49 Mn	22%	Energy £25.5 Mn	36%	Contractors £4.2 Mn	35%

Similarly, the cost structure of the frozen food manufacturers of commodity and added value products, reveals two significant controllable costs: labour and distribution (Table 7.10). Both of these are amenable to immediate reduction through the use of contractors. For example, labour costs could be reduced through the use of temporary or agency labour, or even by using contract packing companies. Distribution costs of frozen food companies are in large part shaped by the efficiency of their cold storage facilities (which is undersupplied in the South East of England) and their location. There are now a number of national cold storage and distribution contractors which have grown to serve both frozen and chilled food manufacturers and retailers.

Apart from the immediate cost savings to be made by the direct substitution of an on-site/in-house service by a contractor, the absolute size of the saving must also be significant, *eg*, £1–2m, or a minimum of 10% of the original budget. The size of the saving is dependent upon the size of the savings required and the time period in which they can be made. Many of the very large manufacturing sites (those employing in excess of 2000 people in the early 1980s) have sought to reduce their costs by at least 30% over a 2–3 year period and have therefore tackled the largest controllable costs in order to achieve immediate savings. Now that many of the larger budgets have been tackled, and in part reduced, companies are seeking ways of further reducing costs and, in particular, raising efficiency.

TABLE 7.10
Structure of Costs for Commodity and Added Value for Frozen Foods

	Commodity Products	*Added Value Products*
Raw Materials	65–70	45
Packaging	5–10	10
Labour	15	25
Depreciation	2	1
Distribution	5	6
Other	2	6
Trading Profit	4	7

Nature of Investment: The size, content and ownership of new plant and equipment can have a significant influence upon the use of contractors. First, there is the absolute size of the investment in particular type of technology and the role of the technology in the provision of the "core" product or service of a company. The more widespread use of a particular technology — *eg*, computer based process controllers in a company — can create sufficient internal demand for the skills to set up, modify and maintain the technology. However, in many small companies the internal demand for such skills is insufficient and so contractors are used (often the suppliers or the manufacturers of the equipment). Second, the rate of change in a particular technology also encourages even some of the largest users of some technologies — *eg*, the Honeywell TDC 2000 and TDC 3000 systems — to make use of contractors. Hence the complexity and the cost of keeping skills and knowledge up-to-date, for a changing (and inherently reliable) technology means that it is cost effective to use contractors. When a technology stabilises in terms of the development of the skills and knowledge relevant to its operation and maintenance, they tend to become internalised by technology's users, rather than its suppliers.[15] Third, the ownership of the plant and equipment is the final key factor influencing the use of contractors. Over the last 5–7 years there has been an increase in the companies in the research database making use of leased plant and equipment. The most frequently occurring equipment being leased is mechanical handling: fork lift trucks, palletisers, cranes, moving platforms, *etc.* As the equipment is owned by a third party, its maintenance is therefore handled by the lessor and not the lessee.

Rate

All of the companies and manufacturing sites in the research database have been seeking ways to reduce both fixed and variable costs. It is the internal and external pressures acting upon the site to reduce costs to survive and to boost profits. The speed of response required varies from industry to industry. Those industries where labour is the largest of the direct controllable costs and where contractors can provide an immediate lower cost substitute, have moved to contractors more quickly. In summary then the factors common to most situations where there has been an increase in the use of contractors are:

- rapid downturn in demand/profits;
- rapid increase in raw material costs;
- low initial usage of contractors;
- company-wide policy of own employees displacement; and,
- failure to win product price increase.

Summary

As regards the overall increased usage of contractors by manufacturing companies the following is a summary of the main factors explaining this situation:

- to reduce/contain costs;
- to supplement low levels of internal resources;
- to comply with a "ban on recruitment" policy;
- to accommodate the introduction of new plant and equipment;
- to allow reduced demand on site for services to be served more effectively;
- to allow short-run increases in demand to be handled;
- to allow training to take place of employees;

- to accommodate the introduction of new, specialist service equipment;
- to reflect changes in plant and equipment purchasing policies;
- to allow overtime levels to be "managed";
- to facilitate the adoption of a focussed manufacturing strategy;
- to make sure of the improved availability and quality of national contractors; and
- to accommodate changes in health and safety procedures.

Conclusion

Since 1981 there has been a significant increase in the use of contractors providing a very wide range of services. From the evidence available from the 238 manufacturing sites in the research database, there are no signs that this trend will be significantly reversed. Fluctuations in contractor usage levels will occur reflecting both the rising cost of labour and the availability of labour. Together these factors affect the comparison between in-house and contractor provision of services. Furthermore, many companies under current trading conditions are more affected by customer service/reliability and quality issues. It is not clear in this changed contractor market if the large conglomerate contractors (often one-stop contractors) are better placed than their smaller competitors to survive and win new business. Finally, it is also evident that the companies do not have a coherent policy as regards the use of contractors and related sources of labour.

Routes used to effect Contractor Usage

The majority of the manufacturing sites in the research database did, and still do not have a policy to continuously review in-house service provision with that available from contractors. One result of this lack of a "contractor policy" has lead to a series of inconsistencies as regards the engaging of contractors. For a start, there have not been a common set of review and evaluation criteria applied to the engagement of contractors in one area, let alone between areas. Leaving aside these inconsistencies, there are two main routes by which contractors have been introduced on to a manufacturing site:

> *Supplementary Route*: Here contractors are used to supplement an existing in-house service on a permanent or periodic basis. The need to supplement an existing in-house service might have arisen as a result of the reallocation of resources

on the site leading to a reduction in the numbers of people devoted to a particular service. The main areas affected are maintenance, engineering and production. Both transport and warehousing usually falls between the two main routes.

Replacement Route: All in-house service can be replaced in three main ways:

(1) Transfer. All in-house personnel are transferred onto the staff of a contractor which has been engaged to provide a service.
(2) Buy-out. In-house personnel and their management come together to form a company which will provide the service they previously provided when employees of the company.
(3) Substitution. The in-house personnel are made redundant and are directly substituted by contractors. Often the in-house personnel might transfer on to other jobs on the site or even join the contractor.

All of these routes have been used on the 238 sites in the research database. The type of contractors falling into this second route are mainly site services, like catering, office cleaning, security, gardening, garage, *etc.*

In addition to these two main routes, there are a series of other factors which have an influence on the routes by which contractors are introduced on to a site, and these are:

Site/Company Contractors: In some areas, like catering, there are economies of scale in the purchasing of materials which encourage the widest possible use of a contractor. Hence, a contractor might be introduced onto a site because it is company, rather than site, policy to do so.
Non-Replacement Policy: Since the main reduction in the numbers employed in manufacturing industry in the late 1970s, a policy of non-replacement has been adopted on many sites. Where such a policy is adhered to, contractors have been used to backfill on a full time (temporary) basis. This "backfill policy" has been adopted in some cases irrespective of the cost implications.
Health and Safety: There are some jobs, *eg*, the removal of asbestos lagging, which are undertaken by contractors on the grounds of health and safety.
Specialist Equipment Requirements: Just as the technology of manufacturing processes and products has become increasingly sophisticated, so has the technology of the equipment

used by contractors. For example, mechanical access and lifting equipment is often required on a site, but not on a day-to-day basis. Hence it is hired usually along with a "driver".

Other factors exist which give rise to the use of contractors which when taken together fall into one of the two routes outlined above.

While it is possible to briefly explain that the routes by which contractors enter a manufacturing site are broadly of two types, there are a wide range of possibilities between the "supplementary", and the "replacement" routes because of the number of people letting contracts and the number of contracts being let. These variations can only be explained and illustrated by means of a series of case studies which are outwith the scope of this paper.

Conclusion

This study of contracting-out of maintenance services in the UK industry has addressed four questions, these questions and the initial answers are as follows:

- *What is the extent and nature of contracting-out in UK manufacturing industry?*
  In all, 117, different contractor services were identified which now employ nearly 60,000 on an annual full-time equivalent basis. These services are mainly provided by 7,000 companies whose business on the 238 sites in the research database is worth £1,544m (1988 prices). Of the 819 largest contractors, 151 were new companies set up post-October 1981.

- *Why has the extent and nature of contracting-out changed in UK manufacturing industry?*
  There are three main groups of factors which explain the increased use of contractors, and these concern: scope, rate, and the selection and usage of contractors. By far the most important factor has been the immediate need of sites to reduce fixed manufacturing costs as quickly as possible. The rate of contractor usage is limited by the scope of the work available depending upon if the work relates to "core manufacturing activities" or to general support services. The latter service can, and in some cases has been, wholly provided by contractors.

- *How has the changed level of contracting been effected in UK manufacturing industry?*
  Two main routes have been used to increase the usage of contractors: supplementary and replacement. In between these two routes there is a myriad of variations.

- *What is the balance between the number of jobs which have been "lost" in the companies which have contracted-out certain services and the number of jobs "created" by the contractors?*
  Over the study period, October 1981 to October 1988, the number of full-time equivalent employees employed on the 238 sites has been reduced by 193,860 (in absolute terms the reduction was 193,608). On the other hand, the number of people employed by contractors on the same site increased by 21,846 (annual average; if the largest seasonal fluctuations are used instead, the increase approaches 40,000).

  On the face of it, the number of jobs lost after taking the increased numbers employed by the contractors is 172,014. It is likely that after making allowances for the size of the off-site use of contractors, the number of contractor employees off-site directly supporting the on-site service (*approx.* 4510), the gains in the productivity of host-company employees, the changes in the capital/labour mix on the sites considered, and the productivity of contractors when compared to their on-site equivalents, the net number of jobs lost falls to about 85,306. The main reason for the reduction from 193,806 to 85,306 is due to the loss of 64,620 jobs (*approx.* one third) due to on-site productivity gains through changes in working time and working practice arrangements. Plus in 1981 the productivity of contractors was markedly higher than that of their on-sites equivalent (in the ratio of 5 on-site employees = 3 contractor employees). So, while the loss of jobs from manufacturing industry has been significant, a large proportion that could be replaced by contractors *were* replaced by contractors (about 43,934, or 34%). At certain times of the year this level of contractor replacement can be up to 50% higher.

It is evident from this pilot study that the extent and nature of contracting-out in UK manufacturing industry is both complex and dynamic. In order to establish the exact extent and nature of contractor usage it would be necessary to examine a series of contrasting manufacturing processes in a series of different labour markets. From the evidence presented in this paper, it has been possible to demonstrate the large industry–industry variation, and also to indicate some aspects of the regional dimensions. Further study would be needed to determine the exact nature of the region dimensions.

It is also necessary to probe a number of related questions as these relate to the efficiency gains to be made through the use of contractors. Is the local labour market more resistant (able to provide a greater number and range of employment opportunities) in which there is a "high" or "low" number of employees employed by contractors? It is to questions such as these that further studies should be devoted.

DR MICHAEL CROSS
City University Business School

References

1 *Department of Employment Gazette:* November 1987
2 *Ready for a Helping Hand?*, BET plc: November 1988
3 *The British Contract Catering Market and its Leading Players*, Gira (UK) Ltd: July 1988. Compass Group plc offer document by Lazard Brothers & Co Ltd: December 1988.
   Contract Catering, Keynote Report, Keynote Publications, London: 1985.
4 Jim Whitson, "Quality Improvement Process. A View from the Chemical Industry", in *Zero Defects. A New British Quality Standard?* A CBI Conferernce Report, Rooster Books, Hertfordshire: 1988, pp 74–85.
5 Ralph Fevre, "Contract Work in the Recession", in *The Changing Experience of Employment Restructuring and Recession*, edited by Kate Purcell, et al, Macmillan, Basingstoke: 1986, Ch 2, pp 18–34.
6 Michael Cross, "Technical Change, the Supply of New Skills, and Product Diffusion", in *Technological Change and Regional Development*, edited by Andrew Gillespie, Pion, London: 1983, Ch 4, pp 54–67.
   Paul Mitchell and Michael Cross, *Applying Process Control to Food Processing and its Impact on Maintenance Manpower*, Policy Studies Institute, London: December 1984).
7 Further details of this research programme are to be found in: Michael Cross, *Towards the Flexible Craftsman*, Policy Studies Institute, London: February 1985;
   Michael Cross, "Raising the Value of Maintenance in the Corporate Environment", *Management Research News: 1988*, Vol 11, No 3;
   Michael Cross, "Are you happy with your contractors, and are you in control?", *Process Engineering*: 1988, Vol 67, No 7;
   Michael Cross, "Changes in Working Practices in UK Manufacturing

1981–1988", *Industrial Relations* — Review and Report: 5 May 1988, No 415;

Michael Cross, "The Changing Nature of the Engineering Craft Apprenticeship System in the United Kingdom", in *Knowledge, Skill and Artificial Intelligence*, edited by Bo Goranzan and Ingela Josefson, Springer-Verlag, Berlin: 1988, Ch 14.

Michael Cross, *Changing Job Structures*, Heinemann: forthcoming, Spring 1990.

8 *Towards the Flexible Craftsman*, op cit, Sections 7 and 8.

9 A Pollert, *The "Flexible Firm": A Model in search of reality (or a policy in search of a practice)?*, Warwick Papers in Industrial Relations No 19, University of Warwick: December 1987.

10 See Mitchell and Cross, op cit, 1984.

11 The term *Contractor*, for the purposes of this paper, is taken to mean those companies which provide their service through the provision of labour on to their client's site. In many cases the labour provided by a contractor is directly substituting for labour previously employed by the client company.

12 These figures are based upon surveys and "expert" estimates conducted by management consultants and in-house staff at Conoco, Shell UK Oil, Shell Chemicals UK, Esso Petroleum and Exxon Chemicals. See also Kelvin Young, "The Management of Craft Work: A Case Study of an Oil Refinery", *British Journal of Industrial Relations:* 1986, Vol 24, No 3, pp 363–380.

13 Nigel Atkinson, "Short of engineering staff? Then call in the contractors", *Process Engineering:* Vol 65, No 5.

14 *Logistics productivity: The Competitive Edge in Europe*, A T Keany, Chicago: 1987.

15 Mitchell and Cross, op cit, 1984.

8
Sub-Contracting and its Effect on Health and Safety

"What are some of the likely effects of the pressure on sub-contractors on health and safety at work and what additional measures are likely to control undesirable trends?"

(1)   Contractors and sub-contractors have always been used in industry. From 1985 onwards with the effects of the industrial recovery, there has been a greatly increased use of sub-contracting across a wide range of industries. Construction is the most obvious example, but the same trend is observable in metals, chemicals, engineering and food. Firms now frequently employ sub-contractors in substitution for their maintenance departments — *eg*, engineering, electricians, building maintenance, catering — which they previously maintained themselves, and indeed many sub-contractors were formerly themselves employed by their clients. In some industries, such as construction, some of the riskier jobs — for example, roofwork and demolition — are regularly sub-contracted.

(2)   There is nothing inherently unsafe about sub-contracting in general. Sub-contractors are companies and very possibly employers, like any others. They come in all different sizes, with the same range of faults and virtues that one might expect to find in any other company. Under the law they are not singled out for special treatment, although it is recognised that they will not normally have direct control over the place where they work. Thus the Health and Safety at Work Act 1974 puts obligations on sub-contractors themselves and on the contractors who have effective control of the workplace. As employers, contractors and sub-contractors must safeguard, so far as is reasonably practicable, the health, safety and welfare of the people who work for them. They must also take account of the effects of their work activities on third parties, including other people's employees. And, as persons in control of premises, sub-contractors have responsibilities for general safety, including for means of access and any plant provided. In practice these requirements mean that the main

occupier or contractor has to consider how his activities might affect the sub-contractor. Failure to obey the law can lead to prosecution, or to a prohibition or improvement notice to compel a particular hazard to be remedied. In general HSE consider the law is adequately comprehensive.

(3) The main difficulty created by sub-contracting is possible loss of control by the main occupier or contractor and the need for adequate co-ordination. This is particularly the same where chains of sub-contractors, each letting off part of the business to another, are created. Positive arrangements need to be made to plan the work of contractors carefully and to brief them before they begin work, and contractors should be included in self-monitoring programmes carried out by the main occupier. This can be, and is, done very satisfactorily by efficient companies. For example, Marks and Spencer sub-contract virtually all their non-retailing activities, successfully, efficiently and safely. Firms tendering for Marks and Spencer sub-contracts are beneficially influenced by Marks and Spencer stipulating various high standards. Sub-contract firms can be accredited to British Standard 5750 (Quality Management) when tendering for work, and this should benefit them with major companies.

(4) Problems are more liklely to arise where the contractor or sub-contractor is inexperienced, or does not put enough resources into co-ordination and supervision. These difficulties stem not so much from sub-contracting in itself, as from the characteristics of some companies involved in it. Where there are a lot of new — and possibly inexperienced — firms competing with each other, there may be an inevitable tendency to cut corners in order to reduce prices. On the other hand, a well-run small firm may have better and tighter management control than a large one that is in less immediate contact with its workforce.

(5) HSE inspectors routinely inquire during preventive inspections about the arrangements for controlling contractors, particularly in hazardous industries. Below are some more detailed examples of trends in particular industries. These reinforce the general view that control by the main company is a vital factor; where it is strong (*eg*, the Food and Chemical Industry) problems can be few; where it is weaker (as in Construction) the difficulties are greater. But that does not mean they are insuperable; the trend in the Molten Metals industry suggests that, with the right action within the industry and stimulated by HSE, improvements are possible.

(A)   Construction Industry

(i) The effective control of site activities is a vital factor in achieving healthy and safe working conditions on construction sites and can lead to the introduction and use of safe systems of work. The effectiveness of the control depends on the relationship between the site management, supervisor, foreman, *etc*, and the workforce.

Degree and trend of sub-contracting:

(ii) Sub-contracting has always been a strong feature of the industry. In recent years, however, the industry has fragmented further, with a growing number of small firms, sub-contractors and casual labour.

(iii) Sub-contractors range from large multi-national companies to one-man operations but in every case, the direct link between the site manager and worker has been broken.

Effects of sub-contracting:

(iv) The reduced direct involvement of the main contractor with site workers means that main contractors are less likely to spend money on training, and this may adversely affect site health and safety. Many sub-contractors are not prepared or do not feel able to devote resources to training.

(v) Many sub-contracting firms do not exist long enough for knowledge, expertise and above all teamwork in health and safety matters to be built up and sustained. In addition, many workers who may be regularly employed move frequently from firm to firm and may never benefit from any organised training in health and safety.

HSE Action:

(vi) The "Blackspot Construction" report, which analysed 739 fatal accidents in the industry between 1981 and 1985, showed that 70% of fatal accidents could have been avoided if proper foresight had been exercised.

(vii) In addition to concentrating on the inspection of the more hazardous activities in the industry, Inspectors are paying attention to the quality of site management and its ability to manage health and safety. They are looking at the level of training and supervision that has been provided, and the precautions that have been taken to prevent accidents. They will pursue their enquiries and any enforcement action to the highest levels in companies which do not measure up to the standards expected of them.

(viii) HSE has identified that it is not only safety management which is a problem, but also the need to ensure that health and safety is an integral part of management on site. Inspectors assess the quality of advice given to managers by safety supervisors where they have been appointed. Inspectors are using as a yardstick guidance produced by the Construction Industry Advisory Committee (CONIAC) on *Managing Health and Safety in Construction: Principle and application to main contractor/sub-contractor projects* and *Managing Health and Safety in Construction: Management Contracting.*

(ix) This change in emphasis in inspection from scaffolds, cranes, detailed in site conditions *etc*, to management training and skills, systems of work, company attitudes *etc*, is designed to ensure that there will be long lasting and permanent change, which will extend over many sites and a long period of time, in companies which do not perform well.

(x) HSE has attempted to make sub-contractors, particularly small firms, aware of health and safety problems by running special inspection campaigns (*eg* the Blitz) and by producing and distributing written guidance on health and safety regulations (a series of free summary sheets and *Build Safety*).

(xi) New regulations are being prepared which would provide for the management and co-ordination of health and safety on multi-contractor sites, increase the number of safety supervisors in smaller companies and amend the site notification procedure to identify sites where there are high risk activities.

(B) Molten Metals Industry

Degree and Trend of Sub-Contracting:

(i) Over the past 10 years there has been a noticeable increase in the use of sub-contractors, particularly in the steel industry which has experienced a drastic pruning, both in the number of factories and staff employed: the number of employees in the industry has been reduced by two-thirds. This has led to a much greater use of sub-contractors not only to fulfil the traditional needs, but also for routine maintenance tasks, cleaning services and even operational functions.

(ii) The extent of sub-contracting is difficult to gauge but as an example, at a large modern integrated steelworks with a workforce of 4,500, about 500 contractors would be on site at any one time and during the annual shutdown, this could rise to 2,000.

Effect of Sub-Contracting:

(iii) The increased use of sub-contractors has resulted in health and safety problems similar to those in the construction industry. During 1987, seven out of nine fatalities in one sector of the industry were to sub-contractors. In almost all these cases, the primary cause was lack of control and supervision.

HSE Action:

(iv) Following the fatal accidents in 1987, the Molten Metals National Industry Group (NIG) set up a joint National Working party with the sector of the industry concerned, to review and make recommendations for the safe use of contractors. The review is continuing but the results so far have been encouraging: in 1988 there were four fatalities (two contractors) and an overall reduction in total number of accidents.

(v) Contractors are visited on site as part of an inspection visit and HSE takes enforcement action against companies or contractors where necessary.

General:

(vi) Many large factories now have formal systems for the employment of contractors which may include:

- the selection of contractors from an "approved" list;
- briefing on necessary safety standards to be achieved, and perusal of safety policies before tendering;
- spot-checks during the contract;
- appointment of site engineers to supervise the contract.

(C)   Food Industry

Degree and Trend of Sub-Contracting:

(i) The food industry has not shown such a marked trend to reduce direct labour and employ sub-contractors as the construction industry, but there has been an increase in sub-contracted cleaning work carried out at the end of a normal shift production in the evening or during the night.

(ii) The Food NIG organised a survey of all maintenance and cleaning work in 147 selected factories in 1986/87 and returns showed that contractors were used in the following percentage of firms.

Cleaning	35%
Maintenance	37%
Disinfection/pest control	80%
Other	33%

(iii) Because of hygiene considerations, the work of sub-contractors is liable to be carefully monitored by management, and rules for sub-contractors to work to are more likely to be laid down. Unsafe or unhygienic work by sub-contractors would not be tolerated — protective clothing is worn and there is close supervision.

HSE Action:

(iv) HSE Inspectors check safety and welfare provisions for all cleaning shifts during preventive inspection visits, including "out of hours" visits where possible.

(D) Chemical Industry

Degree of Sub-Contracting:

(i) In the chemical industry as in other industries, building and electrical sub-contractors are used routinely. However, many contractors are experts in their own fields: *eg*, plant installers, instrumentation suppliers, computer suppliers, *etc*. Many are frequently or permanently on site.

(ii) Site occupiers tend to exercise close control and often have specific procedures for dealing with contractors to require them to work in accordance with the occupier's own permit to work system.

HSE Action:

(iii) The Chemical Manufacturing NIG is in contact with the British Chemical Engineering Contractors Association. Sub-contractors are inspected when found during routine inspection and special visits are also paid if it is known that a chemical company is engaging a contractor during a shut-down period. The potential problems of using sub-contractors are well known and are routinely discussed at inspection visits.

The Health and Safety Executive

9

Selecting and Managing Sub-Contractors and Suppliers: An Industrial Perspective

Introduction

All industrial companies necessarily obtain either material or services from external agencies or companies as part of their normal business activities. There are no exceptions to this and it is common for the value of the bought in goods or services to exceed the value added to the product or service by the "user" company.[1] User companies may chose to obtain goods or services externally for a variety of reasons, such as flexibility of supply, or simply because such purchased goods and services are outwith the scope of the user companies' business activities. The experience has very much been that the nature of the relationship between user organisations, and those who supply them with goods and services, is almost always determined and driven by the behaviour of the user organisations. This paper tries to explore current industrial practice in the selection and management of those who supply such goods or services by the consuming or "user" companies, and the subsequent responses and behaviour of those supplying the goods or services.

What do the user's want?

User company behaviour towards its suppliers of goods and services is determined largely by the economics of the situation. A user company will determine its needs in terms of the specification of particular goods or services, and then seek to obtain this product or service specification from the available suppliers. Given that the user company can readily identify all the possible available suppliers of the specified goods or services, there are three important criteria which govern the choice or selection of the particular supplier. These are, in no particular order:

(1) the *price* paid by the user organisation for the goods and services provided;

(2) the *quality* performance of the supplier, or his ability to provide goods or services which actually conform to the specification of the product or service required by the user; and

(3) the *availability* and delivery performance of the supplier in terms of when he will be able to supply the goods or services required.

Before looking at the how these parameters are managed, and the subsequent effects of how users behave towards their suppliers, it may be useful to dwell briefly on the importance of these parameters to typical industrial organisations.

The price paid for raw material typically accounts for some 40%[2] of the direct costs of manufacture in British manufacturing industry; and in many hi-tech assemblers of complex products like electronic capital and consumer goods and motor vehicles, the price paid for bought in material can account for over 80% of direct manufacturing cost. Retailers have equally high proportions of their costs associated with the goods they buy in, and many civil engineering contractors incur almost all their costs through the sub-contracting of work and services to outside agencies.

The quality and delivery performance of sub-contractors and suppliers has equally important economic effects on industrial organisations. Poor quality performance from suppliers will result in poor quality raw material being incorporated or used in the user company's products, resulting either in scrap or rework in the user's process as the product quality is checked or, even worse, the poor quality material and product will be passed onto the user's customers with all that that means in terms of customer satisfaction and market reputation. Clearly much of these effects can be eliminated by simply checking the material as it comes into the user's manufacturing process, but this is an additional cost over and above the price paid for the material. Any material rejected by such incoming inspection may well leave the user company with insufficient material for its requirements, and so compromise its delivery schedules and disrupt its internal production schedules. Poor delivery performance by the supplier will have the same effect on external and internal schedules. Many industrial organisations have historically tried to avoid these disruptions by holding a (very large[3]) "buffer" stock of such material to cover for the poor performance of their suppliers. Poor sub-contractor quality and delivery performance in the provision of services will equally have effects on the user company's quality and delivery performance to its final customers, with the additional point that no stock or inventory of such services can normally be held to overcome these problems.

It has always been relatively simple to quantify the effects of supplier or sub-contractor price performance, and very much less so the effects of poor quality and delivery performance. Current thinking in most industrial organisations, and certainly in those who compete against world class competitors like the Japanese, is that the effects of poor quality and delivery performance are much more significant than those of price performance. What follows tries to demonstrate that the pursuit of supplier price performance almost always has inherent implications for quality and delivery performance, and that those organisations who must compete against the best in the world are actively pursuing, albeit not without some difficulty, the selection and management of suppliers to achieve good quality and delivery performance rather than price performance.

The lowest price available?

Obtaining the lowest price available from those suppliers who can provide the goods or services required by the user company, is normally done by "shopping around" for the lowest price and then selecting that supplier on the basis of his price. Other methods to get a low price, like buying in bulk to obtain volume discounts, are also used, but extreme behaviour here results in high inventory holding costs and is not common except for basic commodities. 'Shopping around" is normally taken a step further in industrial situations, where one supplier is played off against the other so as to drive the price even lower than an innocent enquiry would produce. Needless to say such a policy involves a substantial purchasing effort from the user company in terms of seeking out the suppliers, identifying those with the lowest prices and, if possible, subsequent negotiations to drive price even lower. Such a purchasing policy has been found to have a number of inherent features which can often produce poor quality and delivery performance, but it will always give the lowest price available.

Poor quality and delivery performance results from a "shopping around" policy for a number of reasons. The relationship with the supplier is almost always a short term one because in the pricing merry-go-round it is rarely the same supplier who ends up with the lowest price; indeed many suppliers with few orders will cut prices to the bone to secure work and then increase them to choke off the resulting demand from users. Such a short term relationship can carry with it the seeds of poor quality and delivery performance. For instance, the supplier will not have had the chance to appreciate exactly what the specifications and requirements of the user are, or which aspects of any given product or service specification are critical to the user, and which are not. It is all very well to say that these should be defined exactly in the user's product or service specification as given to the supplier, but they are rarely specified in such a way as to ensure that all aspects of the user's requirements specification can be met. The length of the communication chain in such a relationship is likely to be long in that the product or service will be specified by one group in the user organisation, say the design group, and then passed to the user's purchasing department, then to the sales department of the supplier, and then to the supplier's manufacturing area or provider of the service. Any problems experienced by the operating area of the supplier, where the product or service is actually generated, will have to be resolved through the same lengthy communication chain, rather than direct to the department in the user company which specifies the requirements.

There are other reasons. The short term relationship will instil in the mind of the supplier a relatively low priority in terms of quality and delivery; because almost regardless of his quality and delivery performance he is unlikely to have the lowest price in the market the next time the user is looking for goods or services and so will not secure the order regardless of his current performance. The short term relationship will also mean the user would not advise the supplier of his medium term requirements, there being little point if suppliers are continually being changed to secure the lowest price, so the supplier is unable to plan his resources over the medium term and consequently will often adopt the common practice of accepting orders he is unable to deliver when required by the user. For these reasons and others, where quality and delivery performance in the supply of goods and services to industrial organisations can be a problem, the shopping around policy and the subsequent short term relationship with supplier can lead to these problems becoming apparent.

Excellent quality and delivery performance

Shopping around, as we have seen, can result in poor quality and delivery performance. Many industrial organisations have pursued such a policy for many years and have happily lived with the associated quality and delivery performance. Unfortunately the nature of industrial markets has changed in the past decade and competitors, particularly the Japanese, have developed quality, delivery and cost performance that forces Western companies to pursue ever higher levels of performance, and this has extended to the quality and delivery performance of Western suppliers. A number of Japanese assembly plants operating in Scotland are forced by the common-market legislation to purchase a certain portion of their material from European suppliers, the remainder they can obtain from the parent company in Japan. It has long been the experience of such companies that material supplied by the Japanese parent is almost perfect, defect rate measured in parts per million, whereas material supplied by European suppliers exhibit quality problems necessitating the extensive incoming inspection not required of the Japanese material.

Selecting and managing suppliers to obtain excellent levels of quality and delivery performance involves the establishment of long term relations with a single supplier of that product or service. These long term relationships involve the establishment of a regime of mutual trust and dependence between the companies to enable collaboration to take place to improve quality and delivery performance. It means for instance that the user company forgoes the price opportunities available elsewhere in the market-place and continues to do business with the selected supplier. The basis of good quality and delivery performance from such a relationship is not difficult to see. The supplier will have a high priority to ensure the user receives good quality and delivery performance because a substantial part of his output will go to the user, he will be advised of the user's volume requirements over the medium term and plan his resources accordingly, and communication chains will be shorter where providers communicate directly to specifiers. The nature of the relationship will also ensure that the user's requirements and specifications are fully discussed and identified to the supplier, indeed the supplier may very well collaborate in the specification of the requirements because he will know what is possible and what is not.

The formation of such long term relationships of mutual trust and dependence is fraught with difficulty, and most Western companies are only part of the way down this road. Before the problems associated with the formation of these relationships are examined, it is worth considering the management of price performance in long term relationships, and of quality and delivery performance in short term shopping around regimes. Quality and delivery performance may be monitored in short term shopping around situations by the process of vendor rating, where historical records are kept of supplier quality and delivery performance so as to exclude those with poor performance from the list of available suppliers. Experience suggests that such a method simply eliminates those suppliers who are poor rather than addresses the fundamental causes of poor quality and delivery performance inherent in the nature of the short term relationship, and there are many situations where vendor rating simply causes the user company to more or less exclude all the available vendors because of their poor quality and delivery performance.

It is possible to be more positive on the management of price in long term relationships, though it must be accepted that it will *always* be possible to obtain the material or service required at a cheaper price than that obtained from the supplier in the long term relationship. As has been said before, the improved quality and delivery performance exhibited by such a relationship leads to greater overall economic benefits, though there are methods available to control price performance in some situations. In manufacturing, the methods adopted are that the specification of the product or service required by the user company is examined by both the user and the supplier to identify where the costs are incurred, and collaboration takes place to redefine the product or service specification required in such a way so that it still meets the essential needs of the user, but can be more cheaply or effectively provided by the supplier. Value analysis is the basis of this methodology and the main point is that such processes are very much easier to carry out in a long term relationship where access to the costs of providing the goods or service and collaboration between the parties can readily be achieved.

Problems and milestones in the formation of long term relationships

Current practice in those industries trying to achieve excellent performance from their suppliers, historically more so in the acquisition of goods rather than services and sub-contracting, is that the benefits of such relationships are widely perceived to be worth achieving, but that the formation of the necessary mutual trust and dependence between the user and supplier companies is particularly difficult to achieve. Considerable efforts are currently being made to overcome these difficulties in order to realise the considerable benefits and performance needed to compete effectively. It is easier to see the problems by first looking at the stages of evolution of a long term relationship from that of shopping around.

The stages outlined below are not definite, but outline the major differences in behaviour towards the suppliers from the user companies. The final stages in the process are not evident in the UK and are developed from Japanese practice. It should be noted again that the final goal is the establishment of mutual trust and dependence between the companies to facilitate the many forms of collaborative improvement needed to secure excellent quality and delivery performance.

Stage (1) *Shopping around mode:* Almost no mutual trust and dependence. User companies will also spread orders over a number of suppliers to ensure some security of supply rather than rely on one supplier. Little or no contact with the supplier other than the negotiations over price and the issue of a little discussed specification. Almost universal practice to inspect the incoming material before further processing.

Stage (2) *Preliminary selection of suppliers for long term relationships:* Normally two or three suppliers will be chosen at this stage. The key difference here is the fact that the user company will select on the basis of an audit, or check on the operation of the supplier's quality and management systems at the supplier plant. Successful suppliers will be given medium term commitments in terms of volumes of work, often contractually. Much reduced incoming inspection if at all. Qualification samples to evaluate problems before full scale production. The start of the formation of the relationship where the appropriate people start to talk to each other about their needs and how the problems can be solved.

Stage (3) *Ship to stock and design collaboration:* Further development of the relationships of mutual trust and dependence. The supplier is further assured of his role by involvement in user new product development and the general processes of collaborative quality improvement projects. Investment in the supplier company by the user can be used to further reassure the supplier. Ship to stock from the supplier to the user where, besides having perfect quality, the supplier provides the correct packaging and labelling for the goods to be used straight onto the user's manufacturing process.

Stage (4)   *Product development transfer:* Further investment in the suppliers facilities and the big stage of transferring the product development process for the suppliers part, to the supplier who develops and designs the product to very general requirements specified by the user.

Stage (5)   *Strategic linkage:* The two companies are linked strategically in that as the user's long term product requirements change according to market needs, the supplier is given the opportunity to change his products to suit.

It is not difficult to see the problems. Most of these lie in the perceived mistrust by the supplier of the user company (see for instance[4]), not helped, incidentally, by many years of being beaten down in price by cynical and predatory users with the market on their side. In the ultimate form of a long term relationship, a small vendor must allow almost all of its business to be taken by a relatively large user company. If the user company decides for whatever reason that it no longer needs the parts that the supplier provides, and withdraws, this often means the end for the supplier. It is worth noting that many small clothing and textiles suppliers will not under any circumstances do business with a very famous chain store for exactly this reason. Methods of overcoming these are as outlined above. For the user there are less serious problems of security of supply in cases of supplier collapse, and the release to suppliers of relatively confidential new product development information.

Few British companies have evolved past the third stage of design collaboration and ship to stock, and most are still on the second stage of auditing supplier's systems. Almost none who need excellent supplier quality and delivery performance are still shopping around. The final stage of long term strategic linkage is still some way in the future, if at all.

Summary

For those user companies competing against the best in the world there is an almost universal appreciation that the quality and delivery performance of suppliers and sub-contractors more than outweighs the advantages of obtaining material or services at the lowest price available. This is more to do with the fact that the shopping around process of obtaining the lowest price can result in inherent quality and delivery problems, rather than any tradeoffs between quality and value of a "you get what you pay for" nature. The process of establishing long term relationships with suppliers to improve quality and delivery performance is difficult to do, relying as it does on the formation of mutual trust and dependence between companies, and even the very best British companies have still some way to go before they are equal to their major overseas competitors.

RON MASSON
Napier Polytechnic

References

1 See the Central Statistical Office's *Business Monitor* which gives figures for the purchased goods and services of SIC manufacturing sectors.
2 Average from a major survey of UK manufacturing companies by Colin New's *Managing manufacturing operations: a survey of current practice:* 1987.
3 Case study report of the effects of shopping around, in Ron Masson, 'User-vendor relations in the Scottish Electronics Industry', *International Journal of Quality and Reliability Management*: 1986.
4 A current response of suppliers to the overtures of the users, in Douglas Macbeth, et al, "Getting the message across? Supplier Quality Improvement Programmes: Some issues in practice", *International Journal of Operations and Production Management*: 1989.

10
Ethics and Efficiency:
An Examination of Developing Employment Patterns

In recent years the conventional and accepted methods of engaging, organising and remunerating the services of those who are required to contribute skills, knowledge or labour to an enterprise have been undergoing subtle but significant changes. Indeed some, such as Atkinson, would go further and would argue that the conventional mould has been broken. The doyens of the new philosophy of the "flexible firm", or core-periphery as Atkinson's model is also known, describe a company which directly employs only a core of staff with essential knowledge or skills meeting other needs by use of contract, temporary, part-time and agency workers, the so-called periphery. Such a firm can enjoy numerical, financial and functional flexibility simply by increasing or reducing the total numbers of employed in the periphery, or by altering the mix of skills by dismissing those workers whose skills are temporarily not required and engaging others whose skills are. As a result, it is frequently the case that workers in the periphery will not accrue sufficient qualifying service to allow them to take advantage of employment rights such as redundancy payment or the right not to be unfairly dismissed. As with many changes in society these things have gone almost without public comment and unnoticed except by those employed in the periphery. Therefore in this paper a number of less familiar aspects will be discussed.

From time to time changing undercurrents in society are exposed by traumatic events which may or may not be connected. For example, in the aftermath of the horror of the destruction of the Piper Alpha platform in the North Sea oil fields, a surprised public learned that only 38 of the 167 men who perished were employed by the oil company.

The remainder were employed through contractors, sub-contractors, employment agencies, or in a few cases may even have been self-employed. As the tragedy unfolded it became clear that many of the non oil company personnel were not covered by fatal accident insurance, and some had had no safety or survival training. (The Cullen Inquiry into the Piper Alpha disaster heard evidence that 18 men who died had no survival training certificate.) These aspects of the contracting regime began to come under public scrutiny (albeit localised in Aberdeen) for the first time. This series of articles initiated by Scottish Industrial Mission may encourage an extension of this critical questioning of employment patterns throughout our complex industrial and commercial society.

The following case study is drawn from the oil industry, but concerns one of the most frequently contracted out services in any industry, the catering function. It illustrates the practical and economic implications for the oil company (the client), the catering company (the contractor), and for the employees.

Catering is only one of the many functions performed by contracting companies in the oil industry, and the term encompasses more than simply providing meals: offshore the catering company undertakes all house-keeping duties on the platform or drilling rig, including cleaning, laundry and running the shop and bond.

To understand the development of industrial relations in this sector it is necessary to recall the speed and urgency of the development of the North Sea in the boom period of the mid 1970s. Exploration and development costs were phenomenally high, as were the rewards with oil prices as high as $34 per barrel. Furthermore the pace of development resulted in more than enough work to go around contractors seeking to provide services. It was also a period of relatively full employment. There was competition amongst the catering companies and, being labour intensive, the level of terms and conditions was a significant element in enabling catering companies to compete successfully.

As a result of these factors labour turnover was extremely high (one study gave figures of 150–300% per annum),[1] and there are stories of individuals being poached by company B while waiting to check in for the helicopter to go offshore with company A. Others recall that catering crews were virtually recruited off the streets. The consequent instability had an adverse effect on the quality of the service provided. This in turn had an immediate impact on those working offshore and therefore quickly came to the attention of the oil companies. In an effort to impose stability and quality of service the oil companies put pressure on the caterers to devise a collective means to resolve the problem and in 1978 COTA (Catering Offshore Traders Association) was established. For their part the oil companies, through their organisation UKOOA (United Kingdom Offshore Operators Association), agreed not to accept tenders for catering services from any company not in membership of COTA, though this arrangement was never formalised in writing.

The Association established a grading structure of four grades common to all catering companies. Trade union involvement was sanctioned, if not actively encouraged, by the oil companies and agreement was reached with the Transport and General Workers' Union and the National Union of Seamen on a minimum rate for each grade. (It should be noted that not all COTA companies recognise a trade union; however the collective bargaining arrangements which exist are outwith the scope of this article). Since then negotiations have taken place on an annual basis. However the "COTA rate" was and is informal; at no time has COTA itself ever acknowledged in writing that such a minimum rate exists. Instead it is based on a "gentlemen's agreement".

Until June 1986 the arrangements went as planned with the desired results. Then against a background of plunging oil prices it was announced that a major oil company had accepted a bid from a catering company based on wage rates which were in essence £2,000 per annum below the COTA rate. Catering workers recruited for the new contract, or retained from the previous contract, found themselves facing wage cuts of £40.00 per week. In the months which followed the very existence of COTA was threatened. All eyes were on the next few contracts to be awarded, and had those contracts gone to bids below the COTA rate there is little doubt that the arrangements for protecting the terms and conditions of the catering workers would have collapsed in the harsh economic environment. At the time the TGWU asked UKOOA to re-affirm their informal commitment that they would not accept catering bids unless they were based on the COTA rate. Such a statement was not forthcoming. For a time the terms and conditions of the catering workers hung in the balance of the argument of market forces versus stability and control.

Remarkably the next few contracts awarded were on the COTA rate; the arrangement survived though significantly the member companies of COTA refused to formalise the agreement in writing.

This abbreviated account of the catering sector arrangements serves to illustrate a number of implications arising from this pattern of contracting. First, it can be seen that the pragmatism displayed by the client companies can lead to an unstable and unpredictable environment within which the contractors must operate. Second, in the catering sector and other labour intensive disciplines, the level of employees' terms and conditions of employment is a key factor in a contractor's ability to compete: therefore unless the clients agree to standard conditions (*eg* the COTA rate) wages fall into the competitive arena. Though in a boom period this can mean that employees of contracting companies would see their remuneration increase as clients are anxious to procure essential services and skilled personnel from the contractors, there is, conversely, a downward pressure on the terms and conditions of contractors' employees, especially in labour intensive sectors and saturated markets. In the offshore catering sector this pressure has to some extent been stablised by the COTA arrangements. However in the offshore engineering construction sector there is less consistency.

During "hook-up" (the preparation of an offshore installation for production which can take 18 months or so) an agreement applies covering terms and conditions between trade unions and contractors. It is not signed by the client companies. Once oil production has begun, the agreement ends and maintenance contracts are awarded by a process of regular competitive tendering. Downward pressure comes into play and wages are inevitably reduced. Clearly this, coupled with insecurity of employment (contracts last on average 2 years but can sometimes be much shorter), can create severe problems for individual employees. These are explained in more detail in "The Future through the Keyhole".[2]

Third, the system also creates difficulties for the contracting companies since their workforce requirements fluctuate as contracts are won and lost. These circumstances are difficult to accommodate in conventional employment patterns and as a result new forms of peripheral employment have evolved, accompanied by a proliferation of labour-only agencies.

The potential benefits to clients of this pattern of work can be short-term. In an expanding economy a skilled workforce can become increasingly difficult to recruit and retain, as the offshore industry is discovering. Another major consequence of the tendering process is that individual companies cannot afford to carry adequate training budgets if they are to remain competitive. This being the case, central training bodies such as the Industry Training Boards are particularly important. In addition, the short-term nature of contracts compounds the problem of motivation, loyalty and commitment to the job from a workforce not directly employed and in times of crisis disowned. Hence as a project is coming to an end, clients and employing contractors may find some of their valued personnel moving on to a new contract thereby at least securing another two years of employment for themselves.

The recent movement by client companies in the oil industry to award contracts of greater length (such as four years), and an emphasis on terms and conditions that are sufficient to ensure their contractors are well placed to attract and retain a quality workforce, are indicative of growing client concern.

The catering example and hook-up agreement illustrate inter alia that it is possible to remove terms and conditions from the competitive arena, combining healthy competition with responsible restraints.

Despite the restraints there are however other implications. *ie* for safety — competition is fierce, training expensive. This has led to known cases of men being placed in a hostile and dangerous environment without safety or survival training. This is but one example of competitive pressures creating undesireable effects. The question of ultimate responsibility for these effects and shortcomings will now be addressed.

The client companies argue that their tender specifications include conditions insisting on proper standards for all aspects of the work. For example, contractors must provide their employees with safety and survival training to recommended standards. The contractors however privately contend that the clients pass the cost and responsibility for this on to them, whilst making no concession to such costs when awarding contracts. As one contractor put it, "Bottom dollar wins".

Perhaps the most insidious aspect of the client/contractor equation is that the client companies have successfully contrived to retain control, but at the same time divest themselves of responsibility, a concept not everyone would view as healthy. The question of responsibility in certain issues such as safety must surely extend to the State, the traditional repository of final responsibility. There is no doubt that present encumbents of high office seek to distance themselves from this role, arguing that responsibility for safety rests with the industry. Questions of responsibility must also extend into the employment relationship since the extended development of the core-periphery system offshore and elsewhere has allowed vast tracts of protective employment legislation to be bypassed. For example an employee engaged through an agency has to look to that agency to exercise the statutory responsibilities as an employer; but the agency clearly has no authority, status or even influence in any aspect of the individual's work, other than basic remuneration. It is proposed that the system of employment has outgrown the legislative framework, and therefore new laws are necessary if the State is to retrieve control over matters previously thought to merit it, the protection of those most vulnerable being a possible first priority both from a safety and economic point of view; the placing of responsibility where it properly lies being second.

The growth of peripheral forms of employment has wider social implications. Inevitably the creation of a two-tier workforce of first and second class citizens may create tension in the work environment which will spill over to society at large. Peripheral workers with no pension, sick pay, holiday pay or job security will be resentful of the benefits enjoyed by those employed in the core and will demand change. Politicians will realise that an increasing proportion of the electorate will be "peripheral" and they will therefore become the focus of attention and perhaps manifesto commitments. Eventually society may come to terms with new patterns of employment and an appropriate legislative framework may be developed, but this is unlikely to happen without social and industrial tension and perhaps conflict.

It must be a matter of regret that developing employment patterns which have much to offer in terms of flexibility, efficiency and cost effectiveness fail to ensure that the needs of a significant proportion of employees have been addressed. The COTA example demonstrates that with some safeguards the services of a specialist contractor can be procured on competitive terms, whilst applying ethical standards in setting the terms and conditions of the employees. Such an idea is of course not new, the "fair wages resolution" which used to apply to contracts in the public sector ensured that contractors' employees enjoyed wages on a par with employees in the sector to which they were contracted. The fair wages resolution was removed by the Government in the early 1980s on the justification that more open competition would allow people to "price themselves into jobs". This philosophy may have had some logic to it since people have demonstrated they would rather work for less than be unemployed. The flaw in this particular argument is that we operate in a wider environment than that controlled by the UK Government. With the advent of the single market in the European Community there will be provision for a freer flow of labour between member states. If, for example, the Portuguese were to begin "pricing themselves into jobs" in this country, we would indeed have something of a problem to contend with. Differences in living standards would make it almost impossible to compete. This is partly the reason why the European Commission has included in its proposals elements designed to harmonise working conditions. The thinking behind harmonisation of working arrangements in the Community is similar to the rationale behind the COTA arrangement offshore. If terms and conditions and social benefits can to some extent be harmonised, then these conditions are removed from the competitive arena. Member States can then compete on other factors such as business efficiency, logistics and administration costs without entering a competition based on securing the services of employees at the lowest possible rate.

The logic underlying the harmonisation of standards and the social element that has long been a part of EEC proposals (including the open market 1992) is not entirely based on benevolence or socialism. Rather it is based on a realisation that a policy of encouraging increased trade by relaxing controls, allowing free access and encouraging open competition can exert downward pressure on terms and conditions of employment and such a policy must be tempered therefore by recognised minimum standards. The objective is to have a better system of trade whilst paying due regard to the interests of the individual workers in the various member states.

The UK Government has consistently opposed the harmonisation and social elements of the 1992 package. This harsh logic can also be seen at home where the law is being used to facilitate the moving of services (by insisting on competitive tendering), such as hospital cleaning, into the peripheral area of contracted services, with no safeguards whatsoever for the terms and conditions of employment of the workers concerned. Successful bidders have cut wage rates in some instances from £3.10 to £2.00 per hour and benefits such as pensions, sick pay and holiday entitlement have been abolished or diluted. In order to be competitive, in-house tenders have also diluted the benefits package.

Prognosis

Specialist contractors have long been a feature of any complex industrial scene. If there is a concensus amongst those in control, be it at EEC, Government, client or contractor association level, then proper standards in all respects, including remuneration and benefits to the workforce, can be preserved without reducing efficiency. If there is no consensus, unrestrained competition will inevitably have the reverse effect, with the added danger of social tension, poor safety standards and eventually instability and inefficiency. The fundamental questions remain as always. First, how should work be organised? Second, who should profit and to what degree? Third, who should set the standards for the participants; and finally, what should those standards be?

MEL KEENAN
The Banking Insurance and Financial Union
ALIX THOM
Robert Gordon's Institute of Technology

References

1 James Buchan, 'Approaches and Attitudes of Managers to Collective Bargaining in North East Scotland', unpublished PhD thesis, RGIT Business School, Aberdeen, 1984.
2 Personnel Review: 1988, Vol 17, No 1.

11

Changing Work Patterns: The Consequences of the Competitive Tendering of NHS Ancillary Services

The use of sub-contracting in industry is by no means a new practice and indeed it has proven necessary and effective in many circumstances. However, in recent years the practice has become increasingly widespread in many spheres of industry, both public and private where it had not been used before, a trend which can have wide-reaching consequences on the conditions of employment of the people working for contractors, and often on the standard of work provided. The aim of this paper is to examine the consequences of the contracting out of ancillary services in the NHS which has been introduced by means of the process of competitive tendering.

Competitive tendering has been enthusiastically promoted by the Government in the name of savings and efficiency, the idea being that the cost effectiveness of a service is tested by putting the in-house service in competition with private sector contractors. In theory such a process has the potential to produce significant savings. Indeed in the first round of tendering in Scotland so far, it is estimated that over £12m savings have been made.

However, there is widespread concern about the process for three important reasons. First, there is concern about its impact on existing NHS employees who will either be made redundant or have to work under considerably poorer employment conditions. The second major concern is with the standards of service that will be provided by private contractors. Finally, there is a feeling that competitive tendering is in fact one of a series of developments which is likely to lead to the gradual fragmentation of the NHS in its present form, effectively the breaking up of one very large workforce into a small core workforce and a number of minor "peripheral" workforces. Using the evidence of competitive tendering as it has developed in Scotland, and with some reference to the English experience where the process is more advanced, the paper will discuss each of these concerns in turn.

Health Boards in Scotland are currently in their first round of competitive tendering, that is, contracts have been put to tender

110

TABLE 11.1
Outcomes of Tendering to End of May 1989

Health Board	Service	Contracts In-House	Contracted Out
Argyll & Clyde	Domestic	3	
	Catering	2	
Ayrshire & Arran	Domestic	3	
	Catering	2	
	Vehicle Maintenance	1	
Borders	Domestic	1	
	Catering	1	
Dumfries & Galloway	Domestic	1	
	Catering	1	
Fife	Domestic	1	1 (Initial Health Care Services)
	Catering	2	
Forth Valley	Domestic	2	
	Catering	2	
Grampian	Domestic		2 (Mediguard)
	Catering	1	
Greater Glasgow	Domestic	4	10 (IHCS, Hospital Hygiene, Dysart Sunlight)
	Catering	8	1 (Sodexho)
	Portering		1 (IHCS)
Highlands	Domestic	1	
	Catering	1	
	Laundry		1 (Lairg Electric)
Lanarkshire	Domestic	7	
	Catering	1	
Lothian	Domestic		2 (IHCS)
	Catering	2	
	Grounds & Gardens	4	
Tayside	Domestic)		
	Catering)	31	2 (IHCS Mediguard)
		82	20

for the first time and are now under operation either under in-house management or by private contractors. Table 11.1 summarises the position.

It is important to point out, however, that competitive tendering is an ongoing process and there are a considerable number of contracts currently in the process of being tendered. Most of these are for domestic and catering services, although there is an increasing number of "multiple-service contracts" going to tender, which cover the whole range of hotel-type services used in hospitals and clinics. Some health boards are even considering putting a much wider range of services out to tender. In Forth Valley feasibility studies are currently underway to decide on the competitive tendering of pharmacy, laboratory, X-ray and Medical Records services. However, this appears to be the exception rather than the rule.

Table 11.1 illustrates that the majority of contracts (80.4%) so far tendered have been awarded to in-house tenderers. There are a variety of reasons for this. In some cases the contracts are quite small and attracted little interest from the private sector. In other cases the private tenders submitted simply did not convince the health board that they would be able to maintain satisfactory performance standards within the tender price. In many cases, however, the in-house tender was made sufficiently competitive to be successful, often by severe reductions in input hours, an increase in performance levels and reduced bonuses. This means that significant changes in working patterns are being implemented both under in-house management and under private contractors. However, health unions and the general public are more specifically concerned about the increasing trend towards contracting out, which as the table shows is concentrated particularly in three areas: Glasgow, Lothian and Grampian.

Employment Conditions

In these areas there has been considerable controversy over the tendering results, with suspicion of unfair bias towards the private contractors, and a concern that the private contractors have been able to submit much lower bids largely as a result of the very poor conditions of employment they offer. For example, in the Grampian area the cleaning company Mediguard won two contracts despite the concern expressed by three separate reports about the very low input hours proposed, the level of sickness allowance, the quality of training and the racial equality policy.[1]

With such contractors being successful it is clear that savings have been made at the expense of the already low-paid staff. This was also the case in the first round of tendering in England. One Government publication gives evidence to support this claim:

> "Savings have arisen mainly from . . . less favourable conditions of employment, greater use of part time staff, changes in working practices and increased productivity."[2]

The first important element in the working conditions is the level of pay. Public sector employees receive nationally agreed rates of pay, and under the Fair Wages Resolution private contractors were also bound by these national agreements for public sector equivalent jobs. However, the Government rescinded the FWR, thus allowing private contractors to cut back on labour costs. One contractor in Glasgow is reported to be paying a basic rate of just £1.75 per hour,[3] that is 53 pence per hour lower than the nationally agreed rate.

Even where the private companies offer the same basic rate of pay, the actual amount earned in a week will be greatly reduced as employees are often recruited on a part-time basis. Being part-time this also means that the employees will get fewer paid holidays and will not receive statutory sick pay, as well as allowing the contractor to avoid National Insurance Contributions.

A further change in working practices is the change in shift patterns. Employees previously earned overtime rates for working at weekends. Now the contracts, both in-house and private often include "five and two" shifts whereby the employee works any five days on and any two days off. If the weekend happens to be part of the five it is treated as ordinary working days with no overtime provision.

In Scotland there is evidence that the poor conditions are discouraging employees from taking offers of employment with new contractors. One example of this is Initial Health Care's domestic contract at Edinburgh Royal Infirmary. When the company first took over the contract, they had great difficulty in recruiting sufficient staff, achieving only 50% of their requirements. These shortages seriously impaired the standards of cleaning, and on one occasion IHCS had to import bus loads of staff from Middlesborough, paying them £150 per head per day, to make up the numbers. (NUPE members claim that this has been a regular practice, which Initial deny). The company continued to suffer recruitment problems despite having taken the unprecedented step of putting wages up and introducing a bonus just weeks into the contract period.[4]

Clearly these increasingly poor employment conditions are a result of the commercial pressures on the contractors to make their contract price as cheap as possible. While such pressures exist, I think there should be some form of regulation on the standards of employment conditions offered. A restoration of the Fair Wages Resolution, or some similar legislation, would force competing contractors to seek savings in other areas and to concentrate their efforts on offering the best service for the given price.

Another element in working conditions is health and safety, and this is a factor which is heavily influenced by cost. It is all too easy to cut corners for the sake of making savings. In the case of the health service ancillary services, such short cuts can be very serious. Apart from the danger of infection to patients from badly cleaned wards and toilets, there is also a danger to the nurses, doctors and ancillary staff working in the hospitals. Often accidents can be caused by the simplest of faults, such as poor marking of recently cleaned and consequently slippy floors. (One such accident occurred at Queen Mary's Hospital, Twickenham in 1987 when a pensioner fell on a wet corridor floor and was feared to be permanently disabled.)[5] This is a notoriously difficult area to control and existing legislation on health and safety is often difficult to enforce. The problem could be partially reduced with improved training about health and safety matters, although this too would prove very difficult to enforce.

Service Standards

The second major concern of those opposing competitive tendering is the impact it will have on service standards. This concern is not surprising given that policy guidelines on competitive tendering clearly state that price is the most important criteria, not quality:

> "In no circumstances should a contractor not submitting the lowest tender be awarded the contract unless there are compelling reasons ... for taking such a decision."[6]

We have already discussed the considerable reduction in input hours which puts a great strain on the employees, who are expected to cover the same areas in much less time. This is bound to result in a lowering of standards. In Scotland private contracts have only been operating for about six months and already problems have arisen. The main cause is through staff shortages as in the case of the Edinburgh Royal Infirmary discussed above. It has also been reported that the Royal College of Nursing is continually receiving information from senior sisters that private firms are not cleaning to a satisfactory standard and that nurses are now obliged to do extra cleaning in addition to their own duties.[7]

Such evidence would appear to suggest that these contracts have indeed been awarded to the cheapest, rather than the most effective contractor. In the long run this proves costly to the main contractor, in this case the health boards. When a contractor fails to meet specified standards, then corrective action needs to be taken, and in particularly bad cases the contract will be terminated and the whole tendering process recommenced. In the first round of competitive tendering in England there were many cases of this happening. The Joint NHS Privatisation Research Unit, a research body funded by the 4 major health unions, reported that in May 1987, 63 contracts out of 229 had been found to fail, a failure rate of 27.5%.[8] This has clearly proven very expensive to health boards as in the second round of tendering many services which had been contracted out are being returned to in-house management.[9]

In the light of this trend, and the fact that in Scotland any major problems arising have been with private contractors, the best guarantee the public could have that service quality comes before price would be to maintain the ancillary services as an integral part of the Health Service. However, given that competitive tendering is rapidly becoming an accepted process, there should be some control mechanism to ensure the provision of satisfactory service standards. The only existing control is in extra monitoring of peformance and the inclusion of penalty clauses in contracts. However, I think major improvements could be made in the earlier stage of tender evaluation. At present any redundancy costs envisaged by a private contractor are counted as a "below the line cost", which means that the cost is not included in the tender bid but is divided over the period of the contract and recouped against "savings". Another example of such hidden costs is the loss that will be made on NHS machinery which becomes obsolete or is sold off at rock bottom prices. If these costs were taken into account in tender evaluation then the price of in-house bids and contract bids would be more comparable and more emphasis would be placed on the ability of the tenderer to provide the service to the specified standards.

Fragmentation of the Workforce

The third major objection to competitive tendering is the effect it is having on the overall structure of the NHS workforce. The present Government has made no secret of its dissatisfaction with the NHS in its present form. The recent NHS review, and the resulting White Paper proposing the "opting out" of hospitals from NHS management, is clear evidence of this. Many would consider competitive tendering as simply another method of breaking up the service into more manageable segments. By having support services put to tender, the Government is trying to undermine the idea that ancillary staff are an essential part of the health care team. In the words of David Currie a consultant neurosurgeon in Aberdeen:

> "Of course, the threat to the ancillary services is not really about efficiency or financial savings... The real reason for this piece of sabotage is to prepare the ground for further dismantling of the NHS, and Mr Rifkind has placed the ancillary workers in the frontline because they are the most vulnerable section of the service."[10]

The increasing use of contracting out is effectively creating a series of peripheral or secondary status work-forces. The peripheral workforce is likely to be part-time, with consequently fewer employment rights, and it will become very much less stable with greatly increased staff turnover rates. The long term effects of this will be a lowering in standards, as at any one time there will be a high proportion of new or trainee employees and a lowering in workforce morale as there is less loyalty to the job. This generally leads to poor industrial relations, both between the contractor and its employees, and between contractor employees and the 'core' NHS staff.

A further effect of this fragmentation of the workforce is to weaken greatly the position of the health unions, previously among the strongest public sector unions. The Government welcomes the introduction of private contractors who may or may not choose to recognise existing health unions and who will employ a part-time, largely female workforce, notoriously difficult to organise. This opinion is clearly supported by the right wing pressure group PULSE (Public and Local Service Efficiency Campaign):

> "Instead of having one monolithic in-house organisation providing services there will be a welcome fragmentation and

the natural consequence of that is decreasing unionisation. The unions may continue to have members in the firms involved but competition means that they know there are other companies available to do the job if they go on strike."
D. Saunders, Director PULSE[11]

This weakening in union power will leave ancillary workers increasingly vulnerable to squeezing on their already low wages.

This is clearly a major problem for the unions, and for the employees who could find themselves without the representation necessary to serve their interests. It is because of the increasing use of part-time workers in all sectors of industry that many unions are now turning their attention to the recruitment of that particular section of the workforce. I feel that union organisation is still the most certain way of serving the interests of employees and it is particularly important where the workforce becomes atomised and consequently vulnerable. Therefore, in the case of the NHS ancillary workers, most of whom are NUPE employees, it is important that NUPE campaigns for continued recognition by private contractors, and provides a service that is equally attractive to part-time employees.

In conclusion, we have seen that the implementation of competitive tendering in the NHS has led to an increase in the extent of contracting out in the service. Where services have been contracted out, and in many cases where the in-house bid has been successful, many changes have been introduced which have affected working conditions and service standards. Private contractors who have been successful in winning contracts have done so by greatly undercutting the existing service on labour costs. This usually means significant job losses and reduced wages for the remaining employees. In order to protect the employees from such drastic wage cuts, when they are already among the lowest paid public sector workers, there should be legislation introduced or rather restored, which binds employers of workers in public sector equivalent jobs to pay a nationally agreed basic rate. This would then encourage competing contractors to seek savings in areas other than employment conditions.

The public also require some protection from poor service standards, particularly in the case of the Health Service. While there are current control mechanisms such as the close monitoring of contractors' performance and the implementation of penalty clauses, these are proving costly and can only detect service deficiencies after they occur. A more positive method of ensuring satisfactory performance standards is to improve the tender evaluation process. At present the primary criteria is cost. This often gives an advantage to private contractors who reduce their bid by labour severences and yet do not have to include redundancy payments in their price. If such "below the line" costs were calculated from the outset and bids consequently become more comparable, then the evaluation criteria would be more concentrated on the ability of the tenderer to provide a satisfactory service.

Finally, the increase of contracting out clearly has the effect of atomising the health service workforce, creating two basic status groups: the "core" workforce who continue to be employed by the NHS, and the "peripheral" workforce made up largely of part-time workers employed by private contractors. The effect of this on the peripheral workforce is to put them in a vulnerable and unstable position with poorer working conditions and very little security. For this reason it is very important for relevant unions, in this case NUPE and TGWU, to continue their efforts to recruit part time staff in order to protect their interests.

These recommendations will not entirely solve the potential problems of contracting out, and indeed the best assurance of continuing high standards of health care that the public would have would be in the maintenance of the NHS as one co-ordinated organisation, managed entirely by local health boards. However, while competitive tendering is in operation, it is important to consider these measures which could go some way towards assuring service standards and controlling the extent of the exploitation of low paid workers.

RUTH FLETCHER
University of Glasgow

References

1 *Scotland on Sunday:* 4 September 1989.
2 "National Audit Office (1987) Competitive Tendering for Support Services in the National Health Service, HC 318", London, HMSO.
3 *Observer Scotland:* 23 April 1989.
4 *Scotsman:* 3 January 1989.
5 Putney Guardian Series 18 July 1987 quoted in pamphlet produced by Joint NHS Privatisation Research Unit, *Contractors Failures:* August 1987.
6 DHSS Circular (1983) HC(83)18, "Competitive Tendering in the provision of domestic catering and laundry service": September 1983.
7 *Observer Scotland:* 23 April 1989.
8 JNPRU 1987: *Contractors Failures:* May 1987. (NB: The term *contract failure* is used to include cases "where contractors have been sacked or

have pulled out of contracts, or where there have been substantial complaints about the standard of service they provided).

9 For further details, see JNPRU, *Special Briefing — Second Round Tendering: in-house successes:* November 1988.

10 *Scotsman:* 16 February 1988.

11 Quoted in JNPRU, *Privatisation Bulletin*, May 1988.

12
Concluding Theological Discussion

In Industrial Mission we recognise that the subject of these papers demands the concern of Christians and the Churches. We say this for reasons obvious to those who recognise how significant for people are the many questions surrounding the availability, nature, distribution and rewards of work. The subject is of immense significance in itself and rightly commands the attention of many different disciplines. What may be surprising for some, is the interest of those of us in the Church.

We can state our reason and concern quite simply. We believe that in Industrial Mission we must counter the belief held by many people, both within and outside the Church, that there are two worlds: the world of faith, of religion, of supernatural and spiritual things; and on the other hand, the world in which we live and work and deal with practical and physical realities. Many do believe that that first world is the concern of the Church. They think that while people may have to work for their living and deal with all kinds of difficult and demanding aspects of life, they can find in the Church, a refuge. Men and women buffeted by the rigours and stresses of real life can find there, refreshment, recuperation, comfort and hope. In worship and reflection they think people can be given the strength, courage and vision to carry on. They also believe that the other world, of money, machines, technology and industrial relations, is outside the concern of Christ and his followers.

For us, certainly, the Christian faith is not a set of doctrines, nor a spiritual inwardness, nor a series of commandments, nor a detached religiosity. We believe that Christ calls us to live in, deal with, and respond to the world in which he has placed us. His insights, his view of the world, his influence on our minds and spirits, require us to try and deal seriously with the issues which emerge in the world, and with the mind and spirit of the Christian Gospel. Faith for us arises in, and emerges from, the real life context in which we and others have our daily existence, and where we live out our personal, communal and collective histories.

The realities of commercial and industrial society are not only the meat and drink of human beings and societies, but the basic material of faith. Whatever is the legitimate concern of people: work, wages, unemployment, competition, enterprise, training, promotion, trade unions, women's rights, minority rights, redundancy, retirement or anything else, we see those things through the perceptions gained from the Christian Gospel. It is our faith which drives us into the world, for it is there, not in some rarified other world, that our response to the call and message of Christ can be exercised.

From this perspective we must try and understand things as they are, even although we may not be content with what is revealed. Interpreting and analysing reality requires care and attention and an openness to the truth as it is discerned from a number of different perspectives. As one theologian has said, "People with power, who take or influence decisions, need to be reminded again and again with as much documentation and evidence as is possible, that whenever you are dealing with a problem, there is always more than one set of hard facts." He illustrated it with the hard facts on marketing and product development which must be heeded when establishing a business. "But there are hard facts about social deprivation, bad social morale, and all the rest of it in the area and these are just as much hard facts and are as relevant to the development of our society."

Our publication, which deals with the vital and massively important matter for countless people, namely, changing working patterns, requires us not only to seek and to analyse the contributions on the subject from a wide variety of sources, but also to reflect theologically on those observations and opinions.

When we look back at trends in changes in working practices over the past 40 years in Britain, it is clear there has been a marked difference in employment practices at the beginning of that period compared to employment practices in the present. Most, if not all of these changes, are not unique to Britain, but are to be found in industrialised countries throughout the world. Indeed, we are now truly in the era of global capitalism, and it could justly be argued that the nation state as a concept is showing signs of extreme wear, and it is doubtful if individual nations any longer have majority control over their economies, the shape of industrialism, the behaviour of their labour markets and even the price of their goods and services. Forty years ago in Britain the labour market was tight, unemployment low, and virtually everything that Britain could manufacture was sold. Under such conditions, human nature being what it is, it is clear that people will make every attempt to achieve a number of aims: to secure jobs and careers, to protect high levels of employment, to slow down technical change and progress by continuing to sell current and even old designs so long as the market will absorb them, and generally to slow down progress and innovation. It could be argued that all of this attitude is born out of a natural inclination to maintain the status quo, a natural distaste for change and the unknown, and indeed even a natural fear of the future.

Outside the Christian world this would be perfectly legitimate and understandable, and indeed for the majority of mankind's sojourn on earth, maintaining the status quo has been one of the central characteristics. Within the Christian world it is indefensible, for Christ teaches that His followers are to be, above all, hopeful about the future and not afraid of what it will bring, for the future is God. In the coming of the future God arrives on earth, His Kingdom is established. The present, the status quo, is so flawed with man's inherent fragility, that it is not worth preserving and is merely a platform to a better future. Christian society may therefore be defined as society that welcomes changes, that welcomes the future and sees in its coming the possibility of changing society for good, of redeeming mankind, of building a just and more equitable world, in short, of establishing the Kingdom of God on earth. The natural protectionism of the 1950s and 1960s in Britain, and the innate desire to hold back progress, had therefore itself no future. It had to change, and in the 70s and 80s it did so with a vengeance.

Industrialism and labour relations in the 1950s and 1960s in Britain worked hard to minimise competition, essentially by forming large companies with massive labour forces, huge bureaucracies, serving massive markets but offering a restricted choice to the customer. This was good for job security. Generally speaking, it was good for conditions for health and safety at work. For a while it was good for investors, but it was not so good for customers. At the macro level, the 1950s and 60s placed the emphasis, it could be argued, on people, and in so far as it did, it had the general support of the Christian Church. It could maintain itself while capitalism was effectively restricted to a relatively small number of industrialised nations in North America and Europe. However, once capitalism began to spread globally in the 70s and 1980s, particularly in the newly developing countries of the Far East and Pacific Basin, the writing indeed appeared upon the wall for the labour relations and industrial regime of the 50s and 1960s. Essentially, the cheap labour markets of the newly developing countries enabled them to penetrate manufacturing with low wage economies in such a way as to intensify as never before levels of competition which were to have the effect in the 70s and 80s of driving the older industrial nations almost entirely out of manufacturing, into the service sector.

From Industrial Mission's perspective it does look as though labour relations in the developed countries forced capitalism to look abroad for cheaper manufacturing areas. This had the effect of intensifying competition, which in turn drove the manufacturers to look for new, more efficient, more profitable ways of deploying labour. At the same time there was growing affluence, rising living standards in the developed part of the world, creating a more discerning customer base. As a consequence, a silent social revolution was induced, first in the developed world, then in the newly developing world, and now spreading globally. The chief characteristic of this social change, of which labour relations is only a relatively small, but nevertheless fundamentally important part, is the dualism between the centralising of control on the one hand and the fragmentation of manufacture and day to day operations on the other. The phenomenon has been variously described, but in our view is best described as post-modernism. Perhaps it can be seen most succinctly in architecture. One central cohesive structure hangs together, say a large office block, but in the post-modern mode it is made up of all sorts of bits and pieces of architecture drawn from different cultures, times and environments. There is therefore of necessity centralisation, otherwise the building would not stand up, but there is also great diversity in its various parts, and not a little eclecticism.

Similarly in labour relations, companies seem to be moving to a position where control is in the hands of a relative minority of people, but day to day operations may be fragmented amongst many different plants, perhaps in different countries of the world, each of which is virtually autonomous, each of which may perhaps have manufacturing, sales, research and development, and each of which, of course, is a profit centre. Within the plants, labour relations has moved from the old mass labour force with its mass organisations, to team working, to simultaneous production, to flattened hierarchies and to flexible working practices. In this new environment the Church observes the fragmenting process, the greater choice offered to customers, the flexibility on the shop floor and the new emphasis on working together in teams, sometimes multi-disciplinary. At the same time, we also note that the old sense of job security has largely gone for everyone within the work organisation, from the most senior to the most junior. We also observe that the emphasis has now been shifted away from people, the concern to maximise their job security and their health and safety at work, to an emphasis on the task or product and particularly on the relationship between the product and the customer. Gone too are the days when people defined themselves by their job. Now they are defining themselves in terms of the company for which they work. In these respects, the break-up of the old nationalised industries is not just a function of privatisation, but is a typical example of the fragmenting process affecting the totality of the world of work, particularly in the last decade.

In the midst of these changes the Church is, of course, primarily concerned that people who want to work have socially useful work to do. Man is very much the animal who works, put most succinctly by Pope John Paul II in *Laborem Exercens*, when he wrote:

> "Man has to subdue the earth and dominate it, because as the 'image of God' he is a person, that is to say, a subjective being capable of acting in a planned and rational way, capable of deciding about himself, and with a tendency to self-realisation. *As a person, man is therefore the subject of work*. As a person he works, he performs various actions belonging to the work process; independently of their objective content, these actions must all serve to realise his humanity, to fulfil the calling to be a person that is his by reason of his very humanity."[1]

In addition, we know both from our own experience and from the teaching of the scriptures, that man's nature is fundamentally flawed. "The good that I would I do not: but the evil that I would not, that I do."[2] Consequently at work people need protection in terms of health and safety, and also need to be protected from exploitation, both at an individual level and at a collective level. Such exploitation may range from labour-only sub-contracting, to tax avoidance. Moreover, from the Christian point of view, to encourage people to compete against each other in the workplace is an infringement of the basic Judaeo-Christian teaching to love one's neighbour as oneself.

Historically, people have coped with the difficulty of flawed human nature in two ways: by legislating against the more obvious misuses in the workplace, principally by laying down basic parameters concerning health and safety; and by encouraging people to sink their individual differences and act collectively in, for example, professional associations and trade unions. Since Christians see no likelihood, at the moment, of a decrease in the effects of human sinfulness, we are as persuaded as ever that both of these approaches need not only support, but the active participation of the Church, of individual Christians and of men and women of goodwill throughout society. Although new working practices have introduced a number of interesting features, such as team working and flexible working practices, we are not persuaded that the basic issue of man's inherent selfishness has been altered in any respect, and therefore remain convinced of the need for workers' organisation in the form of trade unions and of the need for humanitarian legislation to continue to protect people at the place of work.

The transfer of loyalty through team working from class and union to the enterprise itself, must be viewed by the Church with extreme caution. Loyalty is only built on trust. Working people placed it in class and trade union because, over a long period of years, the broad labour and trade union movement with all its organisations, from mutual benefit societies, down-town mission halls and independent churches, through retail cooperatives, to craft and workplace associations, earned their trust through the moral and economic protection of individuals and groups in a rapaciously economistic society. The work enterprise has no such historical record. Indeed, historically it has often been associated with the driving down of wages, the minimising of conditions, the laying off of the labour force in response to competitive pressures and the business cycle. In order to establish a basis for trust the Japanese, who are in many respects now driving changes in labour relations, have effectually said to their labour forces, we will virtually give you a job for life, and reasonable conditions and pay, in return for your loyalty. During the past 40 years, large companies in Japan have apparently fulfilled these promises and in return have received the loyalty of the core labour force at least. In other words, team working itself is not enough as a basis for loyalty. Enterprises throughout the Western world must emulate the Japanese basis, or at least offer something equivalent in order to earn the loyalty of their labour forces.

Nevertheless, even if these conditions were achieved, the Church would still view the whole project with some unease. After all, enterprises are themselves, whether at top or bottom, comprised of sinful human beings, and work enterprises have of necessity, as their goal in life, the maximising of profits. In the end of the day, people's loyalty and trust need a worthier locus than that. The highest that secular society can offer is home and family life, and the Church supports this. But it says that even here human beings are at the mercy of their own frailties. In the end of the day our trust and loyalty can only be placed in the one who created the world, who so loved it He came into it in the form of the carpenter's son. Only in the worshipping community, in the community of the risen Christ, committed not to profitability but to the spread of the Good News, is there an adequate locus for people's loyalty and trust. People who put their trust and loyalty, first in the risen Christ, will in turn make good employers and employees, not automatically, because they remain sinners, albeit forgiven sinners, but because they have a wider vision of human existence which goes beyond self-interest and the profitability of the work organisation to the welfare of society itself, which ought, in theory, to enable them to make a beneficial impact on any human organisation to which they belong. Conversely, those who say they are committed to the risen Christ and are neither good employers, nor good employees, and devoid of a wider vision of the world and humanity, can safely be dismissed as living an illusion.

Additionally, because they have an adequate basis for loyalty and trust, and thereby a more mature understanding of these concepts, the followers of Jesus will be people in whom others can put their trust, and on whom others can depend, qualities which are essential to the efficient running of the economic system. At this level new working practices become old working practices, indeed they become basic working practices which will never change so long as human beings remain the way they are.

Furthermore, people who have thus committed themselves to the maker of the world have a basic awareness of being stewards within a world that does not belong to them but to Him in whom they have put their trust. That awareness is bound to give to the Christian at least a concern for the environment. The changes in labour relations and new working practices with their emphasis on the product and the task, thereby of necessity pose a threat to the environment. The emphasis on the task, the service, or the product, is essentially short term and customer centred. The customer, however, is not at the centre of the world, nor is he as customer the custodian of the world. On the contrary, the world is the stage on which his life is acted out, and without which he could have no being as a person. Furthermore, the customer also is a sinful human being who will have an inbuilt tendency to put self-interest first. In the end of the day, the Church, which believes in the beneficent maker of heaven and earth, cannot totally subscribe to the centrality either of the customer or of the task or service or product, but must of necessity point to the centrality of God and His world. Any working practices must therefore be constrained by higher criteria, by concern for the environment; and in so far as they are not centred upon these criteria, then they must of necessity be transient.

With the intensification of competition and the consequent loss of job security throughout the developed world, Christians also note with unease that this is often accompanied by pressure upon people, both to invest in the economy by spending or purchasing, and to enter into substantial levels of debt, not least of which is incurred through the taking on of mortgage obligations. The Church's unease at this two-fold development centres upon the recognition that it encourages people to live even more individualised and self-interested lives. The worry about job and income, coupled with pressure to spend and enter into debt, is bound to shift individual concern away from the collectivity of human society to immediate concerns of family and self. Christian disquiet arises from the knowledge that human society is not just a collection of individuals, but is a corporate structure in which individuals pay, as it were, a proportion of self-interest in return for goods, services and a wide range of social protection. Working practices which effectually erode corporate responsibility must in the end of the day be damaging for human life together, and therefore pose a threat to the peace of mankind. In turn, that which threatens the peace of mankind, even in the longer term rather than the short, cannot fully have the support of the Christian Church. The Old Testament condemnation of usury was not based upon an inadequate and simplistic understanding of economics, but was based on the knowledge that enslavement to others, or to an economic system, was itself a threat to the peace of mankind.

Finally, we observe that fragmentation, diversity, choice and even eclecticism may be the marks of the new post-modern society, and as such the Church as no quarrel with them so long as they do not threaten the cohesiveness of society and therefore its long term peace. Indeed, these changes may also have an important message for the Church, which tends worldwide to be monolithic, homogeneous, and therefore somewhat reminiscent of modernist society, and even of totalitarian regimes. It may be that in the new era of labour relations, technology and customer oriented services, the Church too has to change; has to be more flexible, has to be willing to give greater autonomy at the local level, has to be more willing to accommodate change and diversity in missionary practice and in worship, and has to be more open to the possibility of further flattening its hierarchies and devolving power and responsibility to the local level rather than seeking to centralise it in the historical epsicopal system. While the emphasis on image and spectacle within the charismatic movement may not appeal to Christians everywhere, there may well be scope for the main denominations of the Church to move away from the more cerebral forms of worship and even of outreach to those forms which are more in tune with post-modern society and appeal to the whole person, to the emotions and the heart as well as the head. In the end of the day, the Good News of the Christian Gospel is not a system, is not a rational apologetic, but is a basic appeal for trust, for commitment, in return for which human beings can move through a qualitative change in life, despite present circumstances, to experience a quality of life which is found in no other message or in following any other objective.

HUGH ORMISTON
DONALD M ROSS
Scottish Churches' Industrial Mission

References

1 *Laborem Exercens*, Catholic Truth Society, London, 1981, p. 20.
2 Romans ch 7: 19, *Authorised Version*.

DATE DUE
